Start Saving Now

Start Saving Now

How the Times Are Different For Young Generations and Why We Need To Change the Way We Think About Saving

Perspective From Your Generation

By Jim Spiewak II

This book is dedicated to my parents, Jim and Sheron

Contents

---

[*]**Source:** CRS analysis of the *Current Population Survey*

Part 1

The Times Have Changed, We Need To As Well

Yes, Were Talking About Retirement Planning

No matter what your age, any thought of planning for retirement, it is necessary to spend some time learning the meaning of retirement. Retirement is more than just how much money you save or the incomes you want to live off of – rather it's more about your lifestyle, and the choices you make based on the information you learn, know and implement.

Today, retirement can be the longest stage in a person's life, which is contradictory to any previous generation to walk this great land. Retirement will be a very significant part of our lives and it would be wise to treat it as such. In my opinion, there is a big difference between the actual meanings of retirement for each generation. In the early 1900's, those who retired relied on the few resources they accumulated through their lives and family members. Those in the 1920's had huge problems such as the great depression and wars. Beginning in the mid 1930's retirees relied on the new Social Security system that was brought about after the great depression. The next few decades brought retirees defined benefit pension plans that guaranteed benefits for the rest of their lives. Today the landscape and meaning of retirement is different. The theory of retirement will continue to change, as it has for many decades, and so too will the way we need to plan for retirement. Will our generation (Generation Y) and the generations to follow, do enough to one day be able to retire?

What defines retirement for our generation? Our retirement can be defined as the new problems we will have to overcome such as Social Security and Medicare, longevity of life spans, and reduced benefits from both government and corporate

America. We as a generation are already behind in saving adequately for retirement and even though Americans may be more aware of retirement and saving issues, this awareness has not translated into more people taking the necessary action. Most Americans believe they are saving enough for retirement, when they actually are not.

According to the Employee Benefit Research Institute, the percentage of Americans who are saving for retirement has ranged from 61% to 70% between 1993-2006 and during that same time period 73% of working Americans have said they are either somewhat confident or very confident that they will have enough money to enjoy a comfortable retirement. Coincidently, only 20% of American workers know what age full Social Security benefits are available. Additionally, 40% of surveyed workers said they participated in a defined benefit plan, 61% said they expected to receive benefits at retirement from such a plan. This proves that Americans need help.

Today, the baby boomer generation on average has only saved $60,000 and 40% of that generation has saved $25,000 or less. Americans are becoming more dependent on assistance plans yet these plans will be running out of resources. Americans run the risk of having to work until they are forced to retire due to bad health. There are some huge problems that stem back many decades. These problems need to be addressed, because they are the problems that will surface and affect our generation the most and it is time to start saving now!

The Times Have Changed, We Need to As Well

Time is our greatest asset. The time to begin saving is now, whether you are in your teens, early or mid twenties, the time to learn and act is now. My hope with this book is that you find the information useful and that you become educated and learn something new, to inspire you to take action and plan for the future. You will learn that the time to put your financial future in your own hands is now. Ask anyone, who has not saved enough for retirement, if they would do things differently and all of them would say "yes." Don't make the same mistakes and don't say the same thing when you turn 65. My goal is to open the eyes of our generation and future generations to the challenges we will face and to shed light on the fact that the times are changing and we need to as well.

Oh how the times have changed. One of the few certainties in life is that things always change. People change, corporations change and the way we do things change. Oil goes up over $150 a barrel causing gasoline to skyrocket to $4.00 a gallon and we need to change the way we commute to work and leisurely travel. The price of food increases twenty percent, year over year, and we need to change the way we eat by going out to eat less and beginning to budget shop. Corporations merge and buy out other firms causing the culture to change, thus causing the pay structure to change and the entire corporate landscape to change leaving people without a job. Things are always changing, and that is a part of life. One common factor when things change, is that we have to learn to adapt to our surroundings and make changes ourselves, otherwise we get left behind. When it comes to the topic of saving for retirement, this is no different.

The times have drastically changed and we as a generation need to adapt. This world shows no mercy on the weak minded and planning for your retirement is something we need to begin taking seriously at an early age so that we do not become weak. The main theme of this book is to consider the changes that you would have to make in order to make a positive impact on beginning to plan for retirement. I also want to stress the importance of the drastic hurdles we will have to jump over that no other generation has seen before. What might some of these changes include? It might mean that you start saving $50 or $100 each month and contribute to a retirement account that will grow for you over the next thirty to forty years. It might include setting up an automatic contribution program that instantly makes a contribution each month to your retirement account, making it easier for you. It might include changing how and what you spend your money on. Lastly, the most important theme this book covers is that we must being contributing earlier in life to our retirement accounts. People have obtained great wealth on modest salaries and it is my goal to stress to you that the earlier you begin, no matter what your income is, the more you can accumulate for retirement.

In one of the upcoming sections I will introduce to you what I call the Not so Fantastic 4. It is a series of four immense challenges that I believe will combine to greatly handicap our generation and the generations to come. It will not be these four alone that will make it more difficult for us to retire, but these problems will be the main cause for our generation's challenges and the reason we must change the way we do things. My goal for you in reading this book is to come to grips with that fact that things are changing, times are changing and we as a generation need to change.

What are some of the ways we can change? You may or may not want to make the necessary changes, but I would encourage you to make your own list of priorities and make some changes along the way. Communication is an important part of making changes. If you tell someone you want to begin making changes towards saving for retirement, I am sure they will support you. I have yet to hear one adult criticize a younger person for wanting to open up an IRA or start saving for the future. It will not happen.

The following is a list of things that may need to be changed. This might help you get the wheels spinning to begin making changes, if this is important to you. Going out one less time a week, quitting smoking, reducing your fast food intake, starting an investment club, getting involved with activities at your high school, college or university, paying off your car loan and use what you would pay towards your car payment to an IRA, setting aside $50 a month in a savings account, live with mom and dad to save up a bit or getting a roommate to help with the fixed monthly expenses and ask for help from others. Go to Starbucks one less time a week or get a fish bowl and put your loose change in it every time you come home (I do this every year and have never had less than $200 at the end of the year, it is amazing). Those are just a few of the changes you can make. Again, I encourage you to challenge yourself and come up with a few changes that suit you and your lifestyle.

Here are a few of the ways I have changed through the years and you can use them as a starting point. My first major change was to start paying myself first. I decided it was in my best interest to open up a Roth IRA, which we will discuss later in the book. A Roth IRA is a saving vehicle, with tremendous benefits, that allows you to continually contribute to and save for retirement. There are penalties if I pull money out before age 59 ½ but I'm okay with that rule since I am saving that money for retirement and don't plan to pull it out until then anyway. Some IRA programs allow you to contribute each month on the same day, which is exactly what I set up. The company that administers my IRA automatically withdrawals my contribution out of my checking account, at my bank, and filters that money into my IRA on the same day each month. I receive my paycheck on the 15th of every month, so I set my contribution up to go into my IRA on the 16th, the day after I get paid, which allows me to pay myself first. Before I pay any bills or use any money for entertainment, I have already set money aside into an account that I can't touch, without penalty, until I am 59 ½. This is one of the changes I have made and I hardly realize that money is already saved away. I went from spending the money on foolish things to putting it towards something that will benefit me down the road.

The second major change I made was that I set an entertainment budget for the month. I needed to get my spending under control and this was the best way for me to do it. I decided what amount of money could be spent and when that amount was exhausted, no matter what day of the month, I quit spending on entertainment. Doing this allowed me to control my wild spending. If the money was spent in the first week, oh well, no more fun for me for the rest of the month. It doesn't sound like fun, but again it is part of the change I needed to make. I realized that I one day want to retire and this is a sacrifice I felt I needed to make.

The third thing I did to change was set a budget. I constantly write down my budget and put it in places where I can see it. I write down my fixed and variable expenses, entertainment funds and my retirement savings goals. At first, writing out a budget and knowing how much was being spent on bills and savings was a huge change for me. I felt it was important to know that I was saving and more importantly where my money was going.

These are just a few of the changes I felt like I needed to make in order to get to where I want to be later in life. It is not easy, and sometimes making these changes are not fun. But I have come to grips with the fact that times have changed and I need to change with them too or I will get left behind. It does not take a lot of resources or effort to make these changes. All it takes is a little education, knowledge, inspiration and good ole fashioned will power. People back in the 1950's did not need to begin preparing for retirement in their twenties because they knew they could rely on a pension or Social Security income. Our generation will not live that reality, so we need to begin preparing for it now.

Why not be inundated with information now when your young so that we don't have these problems when it's too late? I once read an article that told baby boomers to do this in retirement: adjust your asset allocation, plot your distributions, scale down your lifestyle, sign up for Medicare, buy long term care. I cannot fail to mention that the title of this article was "5 Last Minute Retirement Tips". Why are we okay with waiting until the last minute to learn these things? Instead, we should set up a plan in our twenties and alter it as needed through the different stages of our lives so that we are not forced to making last minute desperate decisions.

Every day I read articles on subject matter just like this article and it makes me wonder, "Am I the only one who thinks this is backwards?" I understand that if someone has gone their entire life and has not planned, they may need this last minute advice, however, my theory is that if you plan early on, you will not run into this problem. This would be like a professional football team going through their entire pre season and not game planning one play, or one strategy for the regular season. It would be like the team going into the first game of the season with no game plan in place as to how they are going to beat their first opponent. That never happens, but in real life people do it with their retirement planning and it makes me wonder why? It would also be like Jay Leno or Oprah not going over their material for that day's show. These entertainers do not just show up to the studio and go right on the air. They have to practice, rehearse, plan and get ready. Nobody just shows up, and goes by the cuff of their pants when they are doing something important, but yet so many baby boomers have done this with their retirement planning and I can't understand why? It makes no sense and our generation can't think like this.

Many in our generation see our parents living like this and we are programmed into thinking that "we will take care of it later in life." Seldom do we hear about the importance of retirement planning in school. So I do not blame our generation for not seeing how important it is. I could include in this book a thousand articles that I see every day that tell soon to be retirees the "last minute thing" they can do to secure their retirement. But when I also know that the average baby boomer has only saved $60,000, what can they really do with those kinds of pitiful resources? They are unfortunately going to work until they are forced into retirement by old age in which they will live on Medicaid, which anyone will tell you is no real way to live.

Instead of writing articles and spreading knowledge of what can be done at the last minute with minimal resources, let's focus our attention on the idea that our generation should learn about retirement saving early in life, plan for these changes and ultimately take action. By learning these important concepts and saving early, we will be better prepared and will not be worrying that we only saved an average of $60,000. In my opinion, it is my fiduciary obligation to help educate, inform and inspire the young generations to take action.

Time is our GREATEST Asset

It is not our material things that are our greatest assets, rather it is time. When saving for retirement, all other things being equal, if you save and invest for longer, you will be better off. I wish it was mandatory that our generation had to start saving as soon as we get our first job. I also would like it to be mandatory that our parents save for us from the time we are born to the age of 18. Obviously this is not the case, and probably will not be. However, if things don't change our generation will continue on the path of working until we die. If we begin to save earlier in life, then time is truly our greatest asset and we can alter this destructive path we are already on.

I have always said when saving and investing, it is more about "time in the markets" rather than "timing the market." The longer you are saving and investing, the greater potential you have for compound interest to work in your favor. The concept is an easy one, start saving earlier in life, yet so few people do it. Saving earlier in life, potentially allows you to contribute less on a consistent basis while at the same time accumulating more. We as a generation need to remind and encourage each other of this and help spread the word that time is really our greatest asset.

Personal Rollercoaster

Parts of my life have been a wild rollercoaster I do not want to revisit. I went from being on the highest of highs to the lowest of lows. At the age of 25 I had already endured more set backs than most people will in a lifetime. Maybe it is because I take on more risks than most, maybe it was to teach me a lesson early on. I am not sure why these things happened to me, but I do know that I learned from them. I tell you this in all honesty in the hopes that you can learn something from my misfortunes. I am not ashamed of what happened and I hope my story will encourage others who are going through hard times to look at their situation and put the pieces back together.

Looking back at it all, what has happened to me is a byproduct of bad decisions but mostly bad timing, and when these two meet, unfortunate things are bound to happen, which is what happened to me. I am not looking for any sympathy, instead I want to share my story to show that sometimes unfortunate things happen to those who work hard, yet you can pull yourself back together. In my opinion you have not started living until you have lost something. If my life were a boxing match then I have been knocked down in the first round, but have since gotten back up to fight some more.

My investment career got out to a great start and subsequently came crashing down much faster than it ever went up. I have picked up the pieces that are left and am now rebuilding. It would be easy to quit, but I won't let that happen. If this happened to me, it can happen to you. If I can pull myself out of a hole, you can too.

The rollercoaster you are about to read is all truth of my life of the time period between 2005 and 2008. There are many other stories just like mine, but read this and take it for what it is worth. You may get done reading my story and say, "good you deserve everything you got." You may say, "great job picking yourself back up." I don't want to ever hear anyone say they feel sorry for me. I realize I made my own bed and I will have to sleep in it. What I am trying to portray is that if you do have an entrepreneurial spirit, it is okay to take risks, and if things go wrong, learn from it and grow. Take what you learned and build on it. The following is my story.

The saga begins while I was a third year college student in 2005. For years I had been saving up money and doing my own extensive research on real estate investing. There are hundreds of "how to invest in real estate" books available and I decided to make the commitment to buy a house, fix it up and flip it for a profit. I took on this project well before any of the reality TV shows came on the airwaves about flipping homes for profit. I figured the time was right, so I decided to go forward with it. I asked my parents to take out a home equity line of credit on their house. This money was to be used to pay for the property. They agreed to let me borrow the money under one condition; that I make the monthly payments. I was certainly fine with this stipulation and that is exactly what I did.

I knew as soon as I pulled into the driveway the first time that I would buy this one particular house. It was a mess, vacant, and was perfect for what I was looking to do. All of my friends at the time were somewhat shocked that I had purchased the house and was re-doing it. They were also shocked when I told them I couldn't hang out for the next three months. Every extra minute I had I was spent over at the house working. I had family help with the repair work and in three months the house was on the market for sale. Upon completion the house looked beautiful and became the nicest on the block. The house took some time to sell and I actually had to bring down the sale price in order to sell it. A few months later I received an offer and after some negotiation we all agreed on a deal and here is the break down of the transaction. The house was bought for $65,000 and I put $10,000 into the house for repair work. Less than a year later the house was sold for $105,000 leaving me with a gross profit of $30,000. I paid the $65,000 home equity line back to my parents and as promised not one penny came out of their pocket on the deal. The flip was a complete success as many things went my way in order for this to happen.

I was so pleased with the work and dedication I put into the home. I now had money in the bank and a willingness to do it all over again. I continued looking for property and the perfect time and place to do it again. My next property venture took me into the landlord market. I became a landlord for the first time at the age of 23. I took $5,000 and put a down payment on a 3 bedroom, 2 bath house with a remaining loan balance of $83,500. After all my monthly expenses were paid off, I was left with a positive cash flow of about $300 from my tenants. Things were going well and my investment career was off to a great start. I saved the $300 positive cash flow each month and was building up a nice reserve fund. I had very few problems with my tenants and I treated them well and in return they respected my property.

With a little more than $25,000 left over from the sale of the first property I set my sights on buying property in southwest Florida. In the summer of 2005, before my last year of college, I flew to Florida to search the real estate market. The market in Florida had been really hot for a few years and I was looking for a place that I could build, live in for two years, sell and move on. I never had the intention of buying this property just to flip and never live in it. I figured that the timing of the completion of the house and my graduation would be right around the same time. After doing my research and finding a development that I wanted to sink my money into, I signed the paperwork, put up $25,000 as a down payment on my third property, which was a new construction town house with 2 bedrooms 2 bathrooms. The house was truly a beautiful energy efficient home. It is important to note here that I got approved, by myself, for a $251,000 loan at the age of 23 with only $17,000 in income for the year. I guess my perfect credit score, lower lending standards and $25,000 cash in the bank helped me out on that one. Looking back on it now, I never should have been able to get my hands on that type of money. Add this loan of $251,000 to my rental property loan of $83,500 and I had over $334,000 in loans, at the age of 23 on $17,000 in yearly income.

In the beginning of 2007 the house was completed, I had graduated from college, got a good job in Florida and made the move down south. Things were going well for a couple months and then suddenly came the big "crash." I began to read more and more about how the real estate market was slowing down. Each month I was writing a check to the mortgage company while simultaneously the value of my house was going down. It finally got to a point where I was up over my head and couldn't make the mortgage payments. It was either eat or pay the mortgage. Association dues in the community had tripled since when I first moved in and taxes and insurance had shot up too. The time of being flush with cash was now over. The economy was falling into a recession and we were beginning to realize the biggest credit crisis and stock market debacle since the great depression. I had $334,000 in loans to pay back, and nowhere near the type of income to make it happen. This is when I began to realize that things were really getting bad.

After unsuccessfully working with the lender to restructure my loan I came to the realization that I had to walk away from the property and foreclose. With the guidance of professional help I walked away from both properties since you can't keep one property and stop paying the mortgage on the other. This devastated me since the rental property was actually putting money into my pocket each month. I did not want to let the rental property go, but I had to.

At 25 years old, I had already lost everything I worked so hard to accumulate. I had no money, no property and two foreclosures on my record. 2008 was easily the hardest, most stressful year of my life. As unfortunate of a situation as I fell into, there are others out there who are worse off than me, such as those in their 60's and 70's who also foreclosed on their homes and had lost everything. I saw this happen first hand. I remember thinking to myself, "at least I have the rest of my life to pick myself back up again." Some of the people I came into contact with were in retirement, and they had nothing.

Again, I am telling you my story, not for sympathy, but to inspire you. I got knocked down, I lost everything, and it hurt. But what hurts more is not doing anything about it once you get knocked down. In this life we will all get knocked down some way. It is how we get ourselves back on track that defines us.

My mistakes were that I stretched myself too thin too early and took on too much debt in the form of mortgages. I will pay the price for it, but I also believe I failed for a reason. I believe that reason was to share with others my misfortune so that I can educate and inspire. I ask that you read my story and when you make an investment decision remember to be cautious. Always keep in mind that risks are involved. Just because we are young does not mean that we can't take on risks. It doesn't mean that we can't begin to save and plan. These last three or four years have been a rollercoaster, but what I have gained is so much more. I have learned that we live in a different world now. I have learned that people will call me a "failure" and a "loser" while others will call me "brave" and "thick skinned."

This world has changed and we as a generation need to change with it. We will not go through life without failures. How we learn from these failures is what will define us as people. I feel confident speaking on these issues since I have seen both sides of the coin. I have seen major successes and I have seen major failures, and at an early age. The times have changed, we as a generation must change too.

Ask Yourself 3 Questions

Ask yourself three questions when considering setting up a plan for saving. These three questions will help you put into perspective what is important. One of the hardest parts about saving for retirement, especially at an early age, is setting aside this money knowing you will not see it for decades down the road.

Question #1: *Will you need to save for retirement at some point in your life?* If you answer yes to this question, then you are like 99.99% of the world. Unless you are the next Bill Gates, Michael Dell or Larry Page, you will need to save for retirement. Sadly, saving for retirement is not something we learn early enough in life. The habits to a successful savings plan should be implemented into our brains early and often. You need to start thinking that you will one day want to retire and no matter what age you are, saving is a must.

Question #2: *If you have to save for retirement, could starting earlier rather than later, be more beneficial?* If you answered "Yes" to Question #1 than you should also be answering "Yes" to Question #2. We will soon see examples of how the earlier you begin investing, even if it is at a smaller rate, you will have the tremendous possibility of being better off later in life, and you could contribute less over the long run and still accumulate more. Saving properly is all about what you know. If you know that starting earlier could mean thousands of dollars more later in life, wouldn't you want to take the necessary steps to make that happen? Unfortunately, most people do not save enough because they do not start early enough. You will one day want to retire and starting to save right now will only benefit that cause.

Question #3: *Why do most people not save enough for retirement?* The answer is simple; most people do not save enough for retirement because they don't have the knowledge early on enough in life to make a big enough impact on their savings. If you do have the knowledge, you also need the will power to take action. Knowing that saving early in life is vital is one thing, but actually taking action is a completely different ball game. Just because you know you can set aside money and let it grow for forty-five years does not mean you will do it. Or, just because you know eating fast food is not healthy for you doesn't mean you will stop eating it.

People working part time can afford to set money aside. People making $30,000 a year can afford to set money aside. Studies have been preformed that have proven that people would not be willing to reduce their spending habits to better save for retirement. In my opinion that is a shame and that is why most people do not save enough for retirement. If we stressed the importance of our countries problems more and how important it is to save, I truly believe that we as a country would be better savers. All it takes is a little knowledge and will power. People don't save enough because they either don't have the knowledge or the will power to make it happen.

Building Wealth, not Giving Money Away

It is very difficult for the young generations to set aside money and not think twice about it. I know its hard to think about life forty years from now, but trust me, when that time rolls around, you're going to wish you'd put that hundred dollars in a retirement account instead of spending it on the latest gaming system. I understand that saving for retirement is not the most exciting thing in the world. I mean, who wouldn't want to go out and spend an extra $100 a month on fun, gadgets, trips and entertainment? I sure would, but we need to remember that the times have changed and if you want to be able to save an adequate amount of money for retirement, you need to plan early.

The hardest part of my job is to convince my generation that one day we will retire and need this money. My clients almost always say something like, "I get that one day I will have to retire, but I'll wait until later to start saving." Unfortunately, that "later" turns into tomorrow, which turns into next month, which turns into next year, which turns into age 40 - when most American's begin saving for retirement. Why would you save money in an account that you can't touch for thirty or forty years when you can use that money to go buy something now? Well you can, but do you have enough money to buy that gadget and set money aside in your retirement account? And if you do have enough money, then more power to you and if you don't then you are left with a choice. The first choice being, should you buy the gadget or the second choice of should you forego the gadget and set money aside in your retirement account? Which is more important, the gadget that you will get use out of for maybe a year or two, or saving for the rest of your life?

Today, more so than ever, we are consumed by companies and advertisers that do their best to pressure us into impulse buying. We live such hectic on-the-go lifestyles that we don't even have time to pack a lunch or make dinner, so we often eat out, thus spending money. I know because just like all of you I'm living in the same reality. Our generation has cell phone and credit card balances to pay. Thirty years ago these expenses didn't exist. It is the mentality of spend now and pay later that we are use to. But whenever I feel like I am getting in a situation where I am spending too much I sit back and reevaluate what it is that I am doing. I ask myself, is this purchase really worth it? Is the $1,000 flat-screen TV with HD at an extra $100 a month worth it, or would I rather put that money into a savings account for retirement? For me the answer is easy. I can go without a HD TV. Those types of things do not impress me. I understand that saving and building wealth is much more important to me than any HD TV will ever be.

Let's look at this HD TV example and compare the two in terms of saving for retirement. Let's say at age 25, I decide to buy the TV for $1,000 and pay the monthly HD fee of $100. After year one I have spent $2,200 on my TV. Let's assume that I have that TV for the next ten years, still paying $100 a month for service. Over the course of that ten years I would have spent $12,000 on monthly service for my HDTV. If I were to invest that money instead into a savings vehicle that would net me 6% return per year until I reach the age of 65, I would accumulate $159,146. So let's recap. At age 25 I made a decision to buy a $1,000 TV and spend $100 a month on the service for it. I kept the TV for the next ten years and enjoyed it very much. Looking back on it all, in costs and service payments, it cost me roughly $13,000 over that ten-year period. But if I decided that the TV was not important to me and invested the money, both upfront and the monthly contributions over the ten years, and then just letting it grow in an account that earned me 6% return per year, my account grew to almost $160,000 by the time I turned 65.

You need to ask yourself; is what you're buying really worth it? Can you live without it? In my example, by not buying that TV, I have created an extra $160,000 in wealth for my retirement. When you are young I understand that this is difficult to see, especially if you have the money to spend each month on a very nice TV. The $100 a month may not seem like much to you. But if you look at the big picture, you see in this example that by not buying the TV and investing the money and letting it grow for me over a long period of time, I have accumulated some pretty substantial wealth for my retirement. You have to keep reminding yourself that you are not giving your money away. You are setting it aside for later in life when you will need it. You are not giving your money away-you are building wealth. The decisions you make now will greatly influence how you'll live when you retire. While you are young, think about the big picture. The next time you are considering a big purchase, try to visualize your life without it or consider compromising and going with the less-expensive option and investing the rest. What difference will that make a couple decades from now?

Another example I like to use is that of a car. A car can be the biggest waste of money. Too many of us think that society will judge us based on the car we drive and the watch that we wear. To me, measuring your worth by these standards, couldn't be further from the truth. I know several multi millionaires who drive ten-year-old cars, because they could care less what other people think of them. Instead they are saving and investing what would be their monthly car payments. This concept has been described in several books and my advice would be to buy a modest vehicle and pay it off. When you don't have a car payment anymore, earmark that money towards a monthly contribution in a savings vehicle like a Roth IRA. If you take care of your car, it can last for up to ten or more years. I am on year five with my most recent truck and it runs just fine. Being in the financial services field, I get a lot of strange looks when people find out what I drive. I have heard things like, "That is not your car" or "You drive that, I thought you were in finance." I could care less what these people say. They are just words, and to me it is just a car. It is reliable, great on gas, paid off and gets me from point A to point B. While everyone else is putting money into a car dealer's pocket by paying a monthly car payment, I am putting money into my pocket each month. You need to decide whose pocket you want to fatten, your car dealers pocket or your own?

Let's look at another example of the difference made by paying off your car and contributing to a savings vehicle versus not doing so. At age 20 you buy a car and decide to pay it off. Your car payment is $250 a month and you can pay it off in five years. You work really hard and pay a little extra each month and get the car paid off in four years. By the time you are 24 your car is paid off and you hope to get another seven or eight good years out of it. Assuming you do get eight more years out of that car, let's see what you could accumulate instead of making a car payment. You take the $250 a month and invest it into an account that returns 6% per year over the next eight years. By the time you need to buy a new car you have already accumulated (or fattened your own pocket) to $31,872. Now you need a new car and can no longer afford to make that $250 monthly contribution, since it will once again be going towards another car payment. So you decide to simply let your savings grow until you reach the age of 65. By the time you reach 65, assuming that you continue to earn 6% return per year, your wealth would have grown to $194,042. So by simply paying off your car and contributing to a savings vehicle, you have increased your wealth by $194,000.

If having a nice car and impressing people with it is important to you, then by all means, keep fattening your dealer's wallet. But if you want to accumulate wealth for yourself, try making changes in your life that will allow you to do so. These are the reasons there are millionaires out there who you'd never guess were wealthy if you passed them on the street. They don't care if you know that they are millionaires. They know it, their families know it, and they could care less if you know. That is not important to them; what is important to them is that they are wealthy because of their good choices, not because they drive a nice car.

The important factors in building wealth are time, consistency, and determination. The earlier you begin and the more consistent you are with your contributions, the more wealth you can build. The more determined you are, the earlier you'll start and the more consistent you'll be. You are not giving your money away; you are simply saving it for a later time. You are saving it for a time when you will be happy that you prepared early and contributed often. Begin to start thinking that you are not giving your money away, you will use it later in life. Retiring early for our generation might mean retiring at age 75. Some scam artists would like you to believe that it's possible to retire by the age of 55. For some of us, we may even remember our grandparents doing so. But our generation will have to overcome hurdles that they didn't and we will not be so lucky.

If we don't plan early enough, we will work until we die. We will not voluntarily retire; we will be forced to retire. If you are forced to retire, do you think you will be able to live the lifestyle that you want after the paychecks stop coming in? If you are forced to retire due to health reasons, what kind of care do you think you will receive from Medicaid? Let me tell you from seeing a family member live on Medicaid, it is not the best way to live. The times have drastically changed, and we as a generation need to change too.

The Retirement Savings Tree

The retirement savings tree is a graphic that I put together that signifies the four basic components every American should have. When saving for retirement, you need these four components. The four components of the retirement savings tree are:

1. Roth IRA

2. Employer Sponsored Plan, 401(k), 401(b) or Roth 401(k)
3. Emergency Savings
4. Insurance

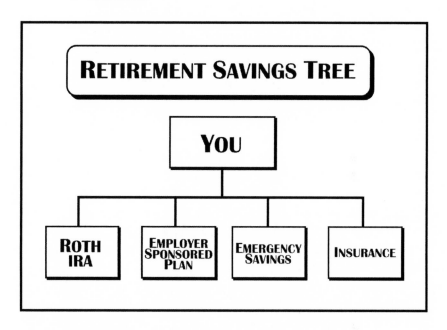

Depending on your situation, your tree may look different, and that is okay. This tree is symbolic of a single tax filer, like one that would be in their twenties. Insurance, in my mind, is the one branch of this tree that is self explanatory, since most people insure their health and their life. I understand that sometimes insurance can be hard to obtain, especially if you are unemployed or work for an employer who does not provide good healthcare coverage. For the purpose of this book, we will focus mostly on the first three components; Roth IRA, Employer sponsored plan, and emergency savings. These three, collectively, are the back bone of your retirement planning. While the insurance is the foundation, the first three are the driving factors.

The savings vehicle that is extremely important is the employer sponsored plan; such as a 401(k) or 403(b) or Roth 401(k). These plans, set up through your employer, allow the employee to contribute a portion of their pre-tax gross income on a monthly basis to an account that will grow tax free. Some companies provide a contribution match or profit sharing program as part of the employer sponsored plan. If this is the case you should invest in the employer sponsored plan before any other to take advantage of the free money. Make sure you contribute the maximum amount to take advantage of the full free employer match. For example, let's assume that your company matches up to 6% of what you contribute into your 401(k). If you contribute 10 percent of your gross paycheck into the 401(k) your employer, by company rules, has to contribute 6%. In this example, assuming you gross $4,000 a month, your out of pocket pre-tax contribution will be $400 and your employer will match the first 6% or $240. This will give you a total contribution into your 401(k) for that month of $640, of which $240 of it was free. Free money should never be passed up.

Statistics have shown that the majority of the workers in this country don't contribute enough in their employer sponsored plan to take full advantage of the company match. In essence they are letting free money slip through their finger tips each and every month, and it is my guess they don't even know they are letting free money slip away form them every month.

The Roth IRA compliments the employer sponsored plan perfectly. Because you contribute to a Roth IRA with after tax dollars, it is not taxed when you take a qualified distribution. The Roth IRA is a key component to saving for retirement and if you qualify for a Roth IRA it should be included in your plan.

I would recommend that each month you set aside some money to an emergency fund. This emergency fund should equal six months worth of living expenses. For example, if you have monthly expenses of $1,000, then your reserve fund should equal $6,000. Be discipline to accumulate your reserve fund and use it only in the case of an emergency; an emergency such as getting laid off, your company going out of business, or making a career change. The Retirement savings tree is a very helpful tool that allows you to visualize what it is that you need.

A Million May Not Be Enough

It is my personal opinion, that saving a million dollars will not be enough to live off of in retirement, for our generation. Accumulating $1,000,000 use to be the American dream, however, for our generation that number will be much more. To have the equivalent of a million dollars forty years from now, adjusting for inflation of 3.5% a year, one would need to accumulate $3,900,000. Our generation's American dream will be to accumulate more than $3.9 million.

There are more millionaires today than ever before. That is not to say they are in a position to retire comfortably. The reason I say that $1 million will not be enough is because of inflation. With inflation, and the problems that our generation will face, $1 million dollars will not even be close to enough to live off of. Taking a look at an inflation calculator and inputting the following data; current age: 25, desired retirement age: 65, desired annual income in today's dollars at retirement: $80,000, inflation rate: 3.5%, we see that an income of $80,000 when we turn 65 would be like someone today having an income of $316,741. If you need $316,741 in income when you are sixty-five just to equal someone in today's dollars (2008) you might need to accumulate a little more than $1,000,000.

Now I understand that generally as inflation rises so too do our wages, but it doesn't always work that way. That is yet another reason why it is so important to begin saving as early as you can. Starting earlier allows you to take advantage of the power of compounding interest. If you think you might need the equivalent of $80,000 in today's dollars, when you are 65, you might now begin to see that you will need to accumulate more than $1,000,000 by the time you retire.

Take into consideration, taxes, medical costs, longevity of life, the lack of Social Security and Medicare benefits, companies cutting pension benefits and these are some more reasons why a million dollars for our generation will not be enough. Our generation will rely on the notion that our incomes will increase accordingly with inflation. We will also have to rely on contribution limits to continually go up through time. What if those things don't happen properly?

Our generation will not have guaranteed income streams upon our retirement. When we reach our "glory days" our generation will have to pull income off of what we saved. Imagine if you had a guaranteed pension income stream to rely on at retirement? That would be nice, however, we won't have it. Imagine a Social Security system where we will get nice benefits from it. Again, sounds nice, but we probably won't have it.

Our generation may not be able to rely on government assistance in the form of fixing the Social Security and Medicare problems. The problems in those two areas are so vastly flawed today, it would take drastic measures for them to be fixed. What happens if they don't get fixed? What happens if drastic measures do need to take place and our generation is forced to make up the shortfall for past generations. You see, past generations may get somewhat of a free ride on our coattails. What I mean by this, is that they paid less into the system than we will and they will get the same of not more of the benefit. It would be similar to a boyfriend paying for his girlfriend's car and he never gets to use it. He is paying all the expenses, the monthly payment, filling it with gas for her, but he never gets to enjoy the car. Now in this situation the boyfriend chooses to pay for everything, and maybe it makes him happy, because it makes his girlfriend happy. But will you be happy if you pay into Social Security and Medicare your entire life and get little if any of the benefits? Our generation could get stuck paying way more into the systems than any other generation and we will see much less in return for what we put in. So if this might be the case, how can our generation expect $1,000,000 to be enough to live off?

The benefits from outside sources for retirement are depleting and the days of the "defined benefit" plans are over. General Motors retirees have a defined benefit plan and all legacy retirees will receive a pension income for the rest of their lives. Those days are long gone for our generation. If you could name me ten companies that still administer pensions, I would be surprised.

The world has changed drastically in the past few decades, unfortunately, people have not changed in the way they prepare for retirement. In my financial planning practice, I would see it everyday. People come up with excuses on why they can't save for the future. They should instead be coming up with reasons why they have to save and save more. The American worker in our country is not even close to saving enough to retire with. We are so far behind where we should be. We need to realize that we are not saving and doing enough to build adequate retirement nest eggs. Accumulating $1,000,000 is no longer enough and if you start early enough you have a better chance getting to where you need to be when you retire.

Try to visualize yourself in the shoes of a 65 year old. If you were 65 today, and had only saved $60,000 (like the average baby boomer) how would you feel? What if you were 65 and had only saved $25,000 (like 40% of the baby boomer generation), how would you feel right now? Putting yourself in their shoes is a tough thing to do but try to visualize what life would be like. At 65 you may not have a mortgage to pay, but you have other daily living expenses. Most notably, you have medical and health care costs, which will be your biggest expense throughout your retirement.

Let's assume that you are 65 and have saved $25,000-$60,000, have a small pension and are receiving Social Security which amount to about $35,000 a year, which leaves you with a pre-tax income of just over $2,900 a month. Healthcare for one person can easily cost up to $1,000 a month. What will happen if you have medical bills to pay? What will happen if you get admitted into the hospital for a series of days? You may be forced to dip into your savings. If this were your situation, you are probably not feeling very comfortable right now. Is this how you want to be when you are 65? It doesn't have to be this way because you now know that the earlier you begin saving, the better off you can be.

4 Case Scenarios

The following is a series of four common scenarios that are typical in today's society. I understand that every person or couple's situation is different, and there are literally millions of scenarios when it comes to retirement planning. There are unknowns such as, becoming ill, fluctuating stocks markets, politics, and taxes. Things change all the time, but we let's take a look at four very common scenarios as to how your retirement planning play's out. Each scenario and eventual outcome will be affected by the decisions each saver makes. For the sake of simplicity, all investment returns in each scenario will be an annual 8% return, compounded annually.

Scenario #1

Saver A is an eighteen year old high school senior preparing for the first year of college. Saver A is excited to live on his own and experience college campus life. As one of the prerequisites for graduating high school, Saver A has to take a short course on the concepts of saving, investing and retiring planning. Saver A is the least bit interested in taking this short class, but is doing so since the course is mandatory.

After taking the class, saver A realizes that some day, even though a few decades from now, he will want to retire. Saver A also realizes that a day will come when he will have to start saving for retirement. Saver A comes to the conclusion that he can set aside $50 a month now, with the intention of bulking up his contribution once he graduates college and makes more money.

Saver A, while at first had no interest in going to this mandatory class, is now a first year college student with a basic understanding in retirement planning, and is already saving in a greater capacity than the average American. At the tender age of eighteen, Saver A has opened up an interest bearing account and begins to contribute $50 a month while in college, using money from his pizza delivery part time job that he works between classes, nights and weekends. $50 a month is an amount that saver A has decided he can afford to set aside and his lifestyle really doesn't change.

Saver A is feeling good about the fact that he is one of a few people on campus that is actually making a positive influence on a big part of his life, retirement. Saver A realizes that while college parties and studying for biology is an important part of the college experience, saving a few dollars into his retirement account is not very hard to do.

Saver A is now twenty-four and is starting his career for a good company doing what he likes, making $30,000 as a starting salary. A few months after graduation, Saver A decides to double his monthly contribution into his retirement account to $100. As soon as he is hired he seeks out information on his employer's 401(k) plan. He notices that his employer matches dollar for dollar up to the first 6% that he puts in. Saver A decides to contribute 10% of his pre-tax income into the employers plan, and as a benefit he is entitled to the 6% match that the company provides.

Saver A now has the account that he opened right out of high school and a 401(k) that he is contributing to. Since Saver A plans on retiring at the age of sixty-five he is looking at forty-one years of service and consequently forty-one years of growth for his two accounts. Saver A realizes that from here until the time he reaches age sixty-five, to retire, he will need to contribute a little more each year to adjust for the cost of living and inflation. Saver A decides to increase his saving 2.6% each year from now until age sixty-five, hoping that wages and income go up that much each year.

Let's now fast forward 41 years and see what Saver A has accumulated. Remember that Saver A is contributing $100 to his account he opened in college (which is a Roth IRA) and 10% of his pre-tax income along with a 6% match from the company, which will all be increased by 2.6% every year for inflation. By the time Saver A reaches age sixty-five, if he earns 8% average per year return on his accounts Saver A will have accumulated $1,918,000. Not bad for someone who only started saving with $50 a month. Had Saver A not saved $50 a month while in school and started when he got his new job out of college he would have accumulated $1,819,000 which is $99,000 less. So because Saver A saved $50 a month while is college, he accumulated $99,000 more by the age of sixty-five.

Can you see yourself doing what Saver A has done? You have the potential to accumulate a substantial amount of money. If you contribute more, you have the potential to accumulate much more. The reason Saver A accumulated $99,000 more by saving $50 a month while in college, is due to the power of compounding interest. He had more money saved up and as his account got bigger the interest he earned allowed his account to grow by $99,000 more. You need to decide if you want to be like Saver A.

Scenario #2

Saver B is a thirty year old woman who has worked for three different companies since she got out of college. Saver B had a hard time finding work that she really loved, but has now found that perfect job and is happy where she is at. Saver B has no retirement savings, but now realizes that it is time to start building a nest egg. She has begun to realize that someday she will wake up and need retirement funds to live off of. Saver B looks into some retirement planning research that her employer provided and learned that they have a 401(k) program with a company match. Saver B learned nothing about saving in a Roth IRA, since her employer does not offer them (no employer can offer a Roth IRA) and her employer has no obligation to educate her on it. However, Saver B is glad to know that the 401(k) she can invest in will provide her an outlet to accumulate funds over the long run.

Saver B has a vision of retiring at the age of sixty, but will work longer if she has too. Saver B also wants to accumulate $1,500,000 in her 401(k) by the time she reaches sixty. By going to financialyoung.com Saver B uses the retirement planning calculators to determine what amount she will need to contribute each year in order to reach her goal thirty years from now. The fact that she has thirty years to save is a good thing, since she will be able to take advantage of the power of compounding interest. But how much will she need to save each year in order to reach her goal? If saver B expects to earn an average return over the next 30 years of 8%, she will need to save $12,000 a year or $1,000 a month to accumulate $1,500,000 by the age of sixty.

At the age of thirty, and in her new job, Saver B is making $30,000 in income, and saving 40% of her pre-tax income is not possible for Saver B. She now needs to decide if she will contribute less, try to earn a better return (which means taking on more risk), work longer or get a second job to be able to afford the entire $1,000 monthly contribution. Had Saver B Started saving five years earlier her yearly savings would need to be $8,000 or $666 a month. The difference is huge and Saver B has a decision to make. Saver B wishes she would have known five years ago, had she started saving, how much less she would have to contribute to be in the same spot at retirement.

Scenario #3

Saver C is like the average American. He is forty years old, in the prime of his career and has not yet saved a penny for retirement.

The average American does not begin saving for retirement until they are in their forties. Saver C has a good paying job, low debt and qualifies to contribute to a 403(b) and an IRA. Saver C is a teacher in a good school district, and has been focused on higher education for himself. He saw little need earlier in his life to do any saving, because for him it was all about getting more education and getting a great job as a teacher, which he now has.

One day while eating lunch with some co-workers the topic of retirement planning came up. Saver C responded by saying, "I don't have anything set up yet, I wouldn't even know where to begin." This got him thinking that one day he will want to retire from teaching and what in the world will he live off of? Maybe a small pension from the school board, but Saver C has no idea what that would be, if any? Now in his early forties, Saver C has decided to start setting money aside in the 403(b) plan. Saver C wants to retire at sixty and hopes to accumulate $1,000,000 by that time.

Since Saver C has waited to begin saving, he will really need to play catch up. Saver C needs to figures out how much money he will need to set aside each year in order to reach his goal. After some analysis on financialyoung.com he realizes his goal of saving $1,000,000 over the next twenty years might be a little out of reach. Saver C finds out he will need to save $21,000 a year and earn 8% per year return on his investments and savings. With the amount of income Saver C makes, there is no way he can afford to set aside $1,750 a month. Saver C believes that he can set aside $650 a month, which is less than half of what he needs to be saving. If Saver C earns 8% per year, he will accumulate $386,000, which is $614,000 less than what he had wanted.

Saver C is in the same position that the average American finds themselves in today. He is forty years old and based on what he can afford to save is just now discovering he will be $600,000 short of where he wanted to be. Saver C now needs to make a big decision. He is $1,100 a month or $13,200 a year short of his goal. Getting a second job may cover the shortfall, and that is an option for him. Saver C may have to decide between working past age sixty or reducing the lifestyle that he intends to live in retirement. Neither option is a very pleasant one; however, for this late saver waiting to start saving negated any other alternatives.

Scenario #4

Saver D is 50 years old. She has wandered through life with little direction and came across some tough spots in her life. Along the way Saver D never paid much attention to or cared about planning for when the day may come where she would want to retire. Well, that day is quickly approaching for her and she has little to show for it. It should never be advised that it is too late to start saving, however; Saver D has put herself in a very tough spot. Her options are limited, but let's take a look at what they are.

Obviously, she can continue working until she reaches a point where she has saved enough or is forced into retirement. Secondly, she can be proactive and start saving. If she has a goal of accumulating $500,000 by the time she is sixty-five she will need to put together a hefty savings plan. If Saver D earns an 8% return per year and saves for 15 years, until she is 65, she will need to contribute $17,000 a year or $1,400 a month. Saver D does not make the type of income that will allow her to come close to saving $1,400 a month, instead she is able to set aside $400. In this example, saving $4,800 a year Saver D can expect to accumulate $141,000 by the time she turns 65. At that rate Saver D will need to continue saving for 13 more years to reach her goal of accumulating $500,000. So Saver D is looking at working until the age of 78.

Because Saver D has prolonged planning for so long, she is left with limited options to reach her goal. Work until age 78 or try to live off of $141,000 for the rest of her life. Chances are she will be forced to work longer then she wanted too. Saver D had no idea that not saving would lead to this and is quite shocked to find this information out. Sadly, the case I just described will be the reality for almost 40% of the baby boomer generation. Due to the lack of knowledge and planning this segment of that generation will work until they are forced to retire due to old age. It does not have to be like that for our generation. We can be proactive and take the necessary steps to accomplish our goals.

The following is a chart of the four scenarios:

Saver A				
Start Age	Retire- ment Age	Years Until Retirement	Savings after College	Ending Value
18	65	47	$ 4,200.00	$ 1,918,000.00

Saver B				
Start Age	Retire- ment Age	Years Until Retirement	Yearly Contribution	Ending Value
30	60	30	$ 12,000.00	$ 1,500,000.00

Saver C	His Goal:			
Start Age	Retire- ment Age	Years Until Retirement	Yearly Contribution	Ending Value
40	60	20	$ 21,000.00	$ 1,000,000.00

Saver C	Actual			
Start Age	Retire- ment Age	Years Until Retirement	Yearly Contribution	Ending Value
40	60	20	$ 7,800.00	$ 386,000.00

Saver D	Her Goal			
Start Age	Retire- ment Age	Years Until Retirement	Yearly Contribution	Ending Value
50	65	15	$ 17,000.00	$ 500,000.00

Saver D	Actual			
Start Age	Retire- ment Age	Years Until Retirement	Yearly Contribution	Ending Value
50	65	15	$ 4,800.00	$ 141,000.00

You May Have Heard Of...

This section provides questions, concerns and other topics that you may have heard of before, but are not entirely sure what it is that they mean. Maybe you have not heard of the topic at all, or maybe you are an expert on the topic. In any regard this section is designed to make you more aware, inform, and educate you on some of the topics related to retirement saving and investing that you may have heard of before. I think theses issues are important to cover at an early age, so that you can prepare and plan for any challenges that may come your way regarding them. It is better to learn them now, rather then later, for at that time it may be too late to do anything about it.

You may have heard that if you save and invest in a Roth IRA you can't access your money until age 59 ½. While this is true most of the time, there are a few exceptions where the IRS allows you to take distributions from a Roth IRA and not be penalized 10% before the age of 59 ½. These exceptions are as follows.

1. There is no income tax on qualified distributions:
   A. after five years
   B. Death
   C. Disability
   D. First-time home purchase ($10,000 lifetime limit).
   E. Distribution for qualified higher education expenses may be taxable, but exempt from the 10% penalty.
2. For purpose of determining a qualified distribution, the five years begin with the tax year for the first deposit (conversion or contribution) to any Roth IRA. However, each conversion amount has its own five year period for determining when the 10% early withdrawal penalty applies.

3. Non-qualified distributions may be subject to 10% penalty prior to 59 1/2 and 5 years as well as ordinary income taxes.
4. Roth IRA distributions generally can rollover to another Roth IRA within the 60 day window, subject to the once every 365 days restriction.

You may have heard that once you begin an automatic savings plan you can't change your contributions. Most plans do allow for you to increase, decrease and even stop contributions at any month, and usually at no charge. You do need to check with your plan provider about all the details, but most plans try to be as flexible as possible because they know that things in your life change and that you may need to make changes to your retirement accounts.

You may have heard that tax rates may go up. This is always a possibility. My question to you is; "Where will tax rates be when you retire?" The simple answer is, "we don't know." Whenever you retire, there is a good chance that tax rates and laws will be different than they were when you were younger. If rates happen to be lower when you retire, then great.

But what will you do if taxes are higher in retirement than they are now? The old way of thinking is that most people's income decreases when they retire. Experts for the longest time have said that retirees will need to replace between 70-80% of their pre-retirement income to live off of in retirement. Because the times are changing so drastically, experts and studies are saying that retirees will need over 100% of their pre-retirement income just to survive in retirement. If this hypothesis holds true, and I am not saying either way if it will not, then our generation should plan on living on a greater percentage of our retirement savings then ever before. My generation may be looking at an income in retirement that is greater then it was when we worked.

What are we to do? You can save your money in the right savings vehicles such as a Roth IRA and a Roth 401(k), early on in life, to plan and prepare for this. This has to be our new way of thinking. We cannot live the way our parents have, it will not work for us. Again, I have no idea what taxes are going to do in the future. What we do know is that we can prepare for the worst and start planning at an early enough age that will allow us to be adequately funded in the proper accounts in the instance that taxes and incomes are much higher when we retire.

The day may come where taxes will go up and we will be forced to pay them at higher levels then we anticipated. If you think about the trillions of dollars in debt this country has accumulated and the funding flaws of the Medicare and Social Security programs, it's easy to think that taxes may go up dramatically in the future. The U.S. is mortgaging our future, which will in turn put the burden of paying back the borrowed money on our generation and the generations to follow. Is that fair? Whether you think so or not, it's out of our hands. It's up to the law makers and politicians, not us, to decide what and when it will happen. You can either be prepared for it or not.

You may have heard that any time is a good time to start a long term investment program. Very simply, the earlier you begin the more you can potentially accumulate and the later you start the harder it will be to play catch up. Because so many Americans wait to start is the reasoning behind why we as a country are not saving enough.

You also may have heard that, timing the markets matters. Most "average" savers and investors listen to the news and get in to the markets when a stock is at its highest because there is a lot of positive buzz about that particular security. The old saying goes, "buy high and sell low." Start to think about investing as *"time in the market,"* not *"timing the market."* When you think like this you take all emotion out of investing. Since no one has a crystal ball, we never know when the right time to get in or out is. Stay invested and in the long term, your savings and investments will be okay.

You may have heard that it takes thousands of dollars to start saving and investing. This is entirely false. All it takes to begin saving is a plan, a few dollars a month and a willingness to stay true to your goals. Many professional advisor and planners do not reach out to our generation because we don't have a lot of money right now. I have given hundreds of presentations to people of our generation and many of the attendees had no idea you could begin saving with very little.

I understand our generation is concentrating on school, starting our careers, paying off debts and juggling many other responsibilities. Most professional advisors do not understand this. They don't understand our situation. Most professional advisors neglect our generation because we don't have the $500,000 account. You see, professional advisors look for the "big" accounts so that they can get paid right now with large up front commissions, fees and recurring revenues. I understand that it is nice to get paid right now, however, the problems that our generation will face are huge and it takes someone from our generation to point these problems out.

Its does not take much to start; you can begin with as little as $100. To accumulate great sums of money, it takes time. The longer you save, the longer you can accumulate, the greater potential you have for your account to grow. It is a shame that very few professionals reach out to our generation. I see why they don't and I see why so many people doubt me for doing so. The nay-sayers say things like "There is no money to be made with your generation" and "Give it up, it's useless and a waste of time." "They will never listen to you." I will never believe the things these people say because I understand the importance of what I am doing, and to me, it is more than just money. I am not spreading this word for "the money." I am spreading this word to help educate our generation.

Most of our generation is not aware of the effects that saving $50 or $100 over a 30 or 40 year time frame can add up to. Again, this is because main stream media does not talk to us about this. But be aware that you can begin even if you don't have a lot of money and that you can accumulate great things. For more on how and where to begin, please visit financialyoung.com, which is a great reference tool and learning guide.

You may have heard that tax-deferral is not an advantage because you will pay income taxes on the gains when you retire anyway. Let's first go over what tax-deferral is. Tax-deferral is simply a feature of an account, such as s Roth IRA, or employer sponsored plans (401(k)).

With a tax-deferred account you get to postpone paying any taxes on the earnings, interest, dividends, and other gains, until you take a withdrawal, which in turn allows you to take advantage of compounding over time so that all of your money continues to work for you. To fully understand and appreciate the power of tax-deferral, let's take a look at a hypothetical example. It shows how money grows when taxes are *not* taken out each year. We are looking at a comparison of two $100,000 investments that:

1. Grow at an annual rate of 7% for 30 years
2. This account is taxed annually (non tax-deferred) at a federal rate of 28%
3. This account grows without paying taxes each year (tax-deferred)

The taxable account (#2) grows to $437,161. Remember this account was taxed each year. The non-taxable account (tax-deferred) grows to $761,226. This figure of $761,226 does not account for any taxes being taken out yet. Assuming that this individual pays a 28% tax rate he will have an after-tax account value of $548,083, which is still $110,922 more than the taxable account. In this example, by choosing to save and invest in a tax-deferred account, where you pay taxes later, you are still much better off.

Many people pay this tax later in life in retirement when they are in a lower tax bracket. So let's assume that the saver who invested in the tax-deferred account (#3) pays a flat tax rate of 20% in retirement; he would then have an account value of

$608,981. So saving in a tax-deferred account can be extremely beneficial. You do have choices as to when you will pay those taxes. Either you pay taxes every year or only when you make a withdrawal. Even though you may have heard that tax-deferral is not an advantage, I would argue that tax-deferral can indeed be a benefit.

New Way of Thinking for Our Generation

If the times are changing then what has worked in the past does not guarantee that it will work in the future. Our parents' generation did things differently than we need to. We need to stop listening to the advice that they received and begin to listen to the advice that will benefit our generation. Furthermore, we need to take action on this advice. Our generation needs to change our way of thinking and open our eyes to the vast differences that are taking place right now and even more importantly will be taking shape in the future. Measures can be taken to prepare for "the worst," if those days ever come. Starting to learn and save earlier in life provides a tremendous advantage in helping you achieve whatever it is that you want to get out of a retirement.

Part 2

What Are The Problems Our Generation Will Face?

The Problems Run Deep

I often use the phrase "sink or swim" which helps me describe to someone if they are on track to saving enough for retirement. If your retirement days are ten or forty years from now, you will either be swimming or sinking depending on how well you plan. Developing and implementing the right plan will also largely depend on your awareness of the problems our generation will face. If you know what the hurdles will be, know the ways around them, and you plan early enough then you will have a better probability of being able to swim during retirement. Conversely, if you do not plan early enough your probability of sinking to the bottom during retirement is nearly a given.

Our generation, and the generations to follow, is at a huge disadvantage. Looking at the statistics of the baby boomer generation we see that the average amount of money the baby boomer generation has saved is $60,000. That is an astonishing statistic and it makes me wonder how the average baby boomer plans on retiring on $60,000? Even more sobering is the fact that 40% of the baby boomer generation has saved $25,000 or less. The fate for this portion of the baby boomer generation is that they are going to work until they die. My question to these baby boomers would be, "How did you come to this fate?" If asked, some would say they "fell on unfortunate times," or that "medical bills ate away everything they had." The number of responses I would get would be vast, but there would be one common denominator and that would be that they did not plan earlier in life and had they did, potentially things would be different today.

The baby boomer generation did not plan accordingly for retirement, however, they have a few safety nets such as pensions and Social Security benefits that our generation will not have. Social Security benefits may be around when we are eligible to receive them, but nowhere near the rate or capacity of the baby boomer generation, which puts us at a huge disadvantage.

I don't want you saying to yourself at age 60, "I wish I had saved more" or "I wish I knew then what I know now." I don't want you saying, "I wish I could turn back the hands in time and go back and start over." The reality is that we will all wake up someday and be 60; looking retirement right in the face. When that day comes you will have to answer to yourself, "Have I done the necessary preparations to retire when I want to?" "Did I start early enough to accumulate what I need to life a comfortable retirement?" "Did I see the challenges coming and prepare for them accordingly?"

You will have to live with the fact that you are either going to sink or swim in retirement. Things can be done to prevent you from sinking. Think about when you are on a boat and heading out to the middle of the lake or sea. You would certainly want to plan and prepare to make sure that the boat is in the proper shape to function. Why would saving for retirement be any different? You prepare and make the proper plans so that you don't sink.

A pilot's most important responsibility is pre-flighting the airplane. The preflight is where all aspects of the plane are inspected before the propeller even makes its first rotation. Before each cross country flight, a flight plan must be filed. This is to ensure your safety and the safety of other pilots. The same concepts hold true in planning for retirement. Why would you not put a plan in place and check your financial pre-flight list? Why wouldn't you be prepared before you sail off?

The majority of our generation can be swimming in retirement. No matter if you plan on being a doctor earning a large salary or a factory worker with a modest income, you can reach your retirement goals with a little bit of knowledge and planning. There will be great problems that we will have to overcome along the way. These problems will come together at the same time, which no other generation has experienced before. We as a younger generation need to instill in our brains that saving is just as important as putting gas in our tank or putting food on our tables. You initial investment can be modest and you can still accumulate a lot if you are saving over the long run. We will all reach the age of retirement where we will look back and say either yes we are swimmers or we are sinkers.

The Not so Fantastic 4

The not so fantastic 4 are four problems that our generation and the generations to follow will run into in our lifetimes. The reason they are so important to understand now is because no other generation has run into all four of these problems at the same time and it is my guess that we will. These four reasons are exactly why our generation needs to adopt the concept of starting to save earlier in life.

The four problems are: The Social Security problem, the pension problem, life expectancy, and out of control medical costs. Each one of these problems will come together as almost the perfect storm against our generation. To combat this we will need to change our habits and prepare much more efficiently, by saving earlier, more often and being more discipline. I understand that it is much easier said than done, but we must try to instill these concepts into our minds. Looking at these four problems we can come to a few conclusions. As a result of these four problems our generation can expect to see a drastic increase in taxes, a reduction in benefits, a longer working cycle and a longer period of time before we receive those reduced benefits. The truth is that almost all of these are in some way are going to happen and they will shape the lifestyles of our generation.

The Social Security Problem

The Social Security system currently in place today (2008) is completely flawed. One of the few ways it can be fixed is by raising taxes and nobody likes paying more taxes. Even if taxes don't need to be increased dramatically, new legislation will need to be passed to fix the state of the system as it is now. The other solution I see fitting would be to make Americans wait longer to receive benefits and when we do, at a reduced amount. Either way, law makers, who coincidently are not in our generation, will be making the decisions that we have to live with and abide by. Law makers are reluctant to bring up this issue in fear that they will lose their public status as a political figure.

If you are unfamiliar with the Social Security system, here is a brief and very basic explanation. Social Security is a government program funded by the U.S. taxpayer. As we work and earn a paycheck and income, a portion of our wages goes towards funding the Social Security fund (FICA). As of 2008 it is projected that the Social Security fund has a trillion dollar surplus. Furthermore, it is projected that by 2020 that surplus will reach $4 trillion. A few decades later, that surplus will be at $0. The reason for this is because the system will have more people receiving the benefits then people paying into the system. If you have more people paying into the system than are receiving benefits or if you prolong the date at which people can begin to receive the benefits, then the system could be adequately funded.

Social Security can begin for individuals starting at age 62. 2008 is the year that the first of the baby boomers begin to turn 62. Individuals can elect to take their Social Security benefits early at age 62 and if they do, it will be at a reduced benefit amount. If they decide to wait until age 66, then the individual will receive the entire amount that is owed to them. The problem lies in the fact that the baby boom generation has over 70 million people looking to receive the benefits. That generation exploded and the population is so much greater than any other generation, which will in turn cause a huge gap in the amount of people funding the program versus the amount of people needing the benefits.

Back in the 1935 when the Social Security program began, for every one person receiving benefits there were seventy people paying into it. In 2025 it is projected that for every one person receiving benefits, there will be three people paying into it. I will not reach the age of 62 until 2048 and by then Social

Security may not even be around. If it is still around, what benefits can I really expect to get out of it or at what age can I expect to begin receiving it? My guess is that my benefits will be reduced, compared to what other generations received, or I will have to wait longer to begin receiving those reduced benefits. I ultimately believe the system will be fixed, but the question remains to be seen, to what extent? You are entitled to your own opinion, but it might be wise to plan on receiving reduced Social Security benefits and at a later age than generations before us.

When the system was set up back in the 1930's it was perfectly suitable. During those days, the system worked and it thrived. The times have changed and the system will need to be altered. I like to refer to the Social Security problem by using this analogy. Think of Social Security as a twig or branch that has fallen from a tree. Someone picks up that branch with both hands and begins to bend or bow it in an upside down U shape. The more pressure that is applied, the more the branch bows. The branch will eventually reach a point where it cannot sustain the pressure of the bending anymore and will snap in half. The Social Security system that is in place today is close to the same fate; snapping in half. The Social Security "branch" has already fallen off the tree, someone has picked it up and has begun to bow and bend it. It is only a matter of time before it finally snaps and the system as we know it will be completely destroyed. The government may step in and make some changes before that happens, but what will that mean for our generation? It may mean that our taxes will be increased. It may mean that other government programs will be ended. The funds will have to come from somewhere, and it is my guess that the burden will ultimately fall on our generation and the generations to follow. We will be left picking up the tab from our parents and our grandparents before them.

We pay into the system every time we get a paycheck. Will we ever see the benefits of that? My best guess is maybe, but I hope that I am wrong. I hope something can be done to correct this flawed system. We as a younger generation need to begin to see that the Social Security system is fatally flawed. Something drastic is going to have to happen for it to be fixed. This is the first major problem that our generation will face as we age and get closer and closer to retirement.

The Pension Problem

The second problem our generation will face will be the fact that we will not be able to rely on a pension from our employer. Generations before us, such as our parents and grandparents, either had pensions or may still get a pension. Let's start with grandma and grandpa. Chances are that they worked for a company for thirty years, had a retirement party and began to receive a pension. A pension is lifetime income for the rest of your life. Corporations agreed to pay you a percentage of your wages during your retirement for as long as you live. Our generation will not have that luxury.

Retirement planning is way different now than it has ever been. Pensions, also known as "defined benefit" plans, are a fading model. Corporations have since switched to what is called a "defined contribution" plan. The difference is that a "defined benefit" or pension plan, which hardly exists anymore, is a plan set up by your employer that would pay you a set figure each year for the rest of your life. The employer is obligated to pay you an income for the rest of you life upon your retirement. The need for the employee to set money aside each month was not necessary, so most people didn't do it. The risks and the responsibilities of retirement planning is all on the employer. Since most corporations do not offer "defined benefit" plans anymore, because they can't afford it, there has been a shift of responsibility and risk to the employee. Our generation will not get a "defined benefit" plan, which means we will only get out of our retirement accounts, what we put into them, and we will take on all the risks and responsibilities involved.

New plans, such as 401(k)'s and IRAs, have been set up to allow employees and individuals to save for retirement, however we no longer can rely on our employer giving us an income check every single month in retirement, like we see our grandparents get.

This book is about seeing into the future and having the knowledge to see what is coming and what is on the horizon. The first two problems that we have discussed; the Social Security and pension problem are two huge dilemmas that our generation will face. We must act differently than any generation has before us to make up for these pitfalls that we will face. In today's world, we will only get out of our retirement planning what we put into it; there are no more free rides. The government and corporate America simply can't afford these "free rides" anymore; it is costing the tax-payer too much. Not having a pension to rely on, ensures the retiree that their only income in retirement will be based on what they have saved through their life. If you plan on retiring, yet have no pension income and little in savings you will be forced to work longer than anticipated.

Life Expectancy

I have a hard time calling this third factor a problem; rather it's more of a concern. Life expectancy rates for our generation, is the third part of the Not So Fantastic 4. Advances in the medical field and reminders every day that we need to live a healthier lifestyle has changed our life expectancy rates. The average life expectancy today is much greater than it was back in the 1930's, 1940's and even the 1980's. This is not a bad thing; in fact it can be good that we are living longer. If we are living longer, then we as savers need to plan earlier to offset our longer life spans. There are very few options here to offset this phenomena and the concept is quite simple. Either you plan earlier in life to save for retirement or you work longer when you get older.

Extensive studies have been done that prove the earlier you begin saving, the more you can accumulate later in life. Our grandparents did not have much of a chance to living to age 90, but our generation has a strong likelihood of seeing a ninth decade. How are you going to fund a retirement if you live into your nineties or beyond?

Consider this example. Assume you retire at 65 and have saved up a nice retirement nest egg because you had been saving since your early twenties. If you die at the 95, which is not farfetched to think, you would have lived in retirement almost as many years as you worked, meaning that you were in retirement for 30 years. If you don't save enough you run the risk of depleting your assets to the point of going on welfare and Medicaid, providing that those programs are still around. Your only other options would be to work longer before you retire or properly plan and start saving earlier and more often during your working years.

We are living longer than any other generation before us. As time goes on, we will find scientific ways to prolong life even longer, which means that we need to prepare even more. The problems are real and unfortunately they are not going away. Know what your options are to prepare for the longer lives we will live.

Increasing Medical Costs

The last leg of the Not so Fantastic 4 is medical costs. Most Americans are unaware of the amount of money they will need to pay for medical costs during retirement. A study was done that shows a 65 year old couple today will need $225,000 in pre-tax savings to cover health care expenses throughout their retirement. Another study was conducted that estimated that same 65 year old couple of good health would need $635,000 in pre-tax savings to cover health care expenses throughout their retirement. Looking at the two studies, we realize that retirees today can expect to pay anywhere from $225,000 to $635,000 in savings just to cover health care expenses during their retirement. If you're younger than 65, the amount you can expect to pay to fund medical expenses will be even higher. Costs for retiree medical benefits have been going up at about a 6% annual rate since 2004, compared to 3.5% for inflation. Even though you may be in your teens, twenties or thirties, this information gives you an idea of the magnitude of dollars we are talking about here.

Talking about medical costs to my generation always is a challenge because most of us are extremely healthy and saving money now for increasing medical costs is the last thing on our mind. I do not expect you to fathom the fact that one day you will need to pay large medical expenses for everyday things like prescriptions, doctor checkups and hospital visits. Please take my word for it that that day will come and one of two things will happen. You will have either prepared for it and you will get great medical care, or you will have blown it off and will receive mediocre to terrible care and treatment. The reason I bring this up is to try to open your eyes so that you see the entire picture of what a true financial plan is all about. You will not need this money for decades, but when you do need it, you will be happy you planned for it. You will be happy that you started early.

Medical costs may be the single biggest cost factor for any retiree going forward. What are we as a society doing about it? The answer is, not very much. Increased medical costs are a hot button issue and many experts shy away from the root of the problem. Medical costs are going to play such a huge role in our lifecycle and so few people prepare for it. Not planning for high medical costs would be like planning on getting married, but not knowing where you were going to live, or how you were going to pay the rent every month or how you were going to get to and from work. That makes no sense. Of course you are going to have a plan in place before you get married. You are going to know where you are going to live, how you are going to get to and from work and how you are going to pay the rent every month. If you didn't know these things then you probably would not make the commitment to get married and live a life with someone else.

It is too late for the average baby boomer, since they only saved $60,000 for retirement. Medical costs are only going to go up. Remember, a 65 year old couple today can expect to spend anywhere from $225,000 to $635,000 on health care costs in retirement. You may have a few years if not a few decades before you see this coming, but what are you doing to prepare for it?

Our generation will face many problems, which will put us at a great disadvantage towards living a comfortable retirement. To recap, we as a younger generation need to safeguard against the fact that retirement planning has switched from a "defined benefit" plan to a "defined contribution" plan. The issues at hand are real and it seems as if they are not going away any time soon. Don't expect to turn your head and hope that someday everything will be okay and the problems will vanish without consequence. Be proactive and take action. The first step is becoming educated to know what the problems are, and then doing something about what you have learned.

Issue number one is Social Security. The system, as it is set up today, is flawed. There is a slim chance that the benefits will not even be there and if they are, they could be reduced to the point that our generation cannot rely on living on Social Security benefits alone.

Issue number two is the pension problem. Corporations simply cannot afford to pay for retiree incomes anymore. As this world becomes global and the business climate consolidates, companies need to shift towards offering defined contribution plans which puts the responsibility and risk of financial planning onto the employee.

Thirdly, it is important to remember that we will live longer. Life expectancies are rising every day and the advancements in the medical field have helped fuel this. If you plan on retiring in your sixties, you need to consider that you may live in retirement for almost as many years if not longer than you worked. Knowing this could be your fate, how are you planning on funding those retirement days?

Lastly, medical costs will be the biggest cost burden on all of us during retirement. Seven out of ten people in this country will need some type of long term care in their lives. I know it is hard to imagine now, at such an early age, but you need to save for medical costs that you will use in your seventies and beyond, because that day will come.

You may have the mind set of, "I'll cross that bridge when I get there," and that is fine. But if you truly want to set up a plan, it would not take a lot of money to do so, maybe $50 a month. I think you will truly thank yourself when that day comes. I have witnessed other generations deplete all their assets and be forced to depend on other forms of income to for daily living expenses, and it is not a pleasant experience. Decide early on in life if you want that to be your fate. If you don't want this to be your fate, you can be proactive and do something about the problems our generation will face. You can't fix something if you don't know what the problem is. The problems are not going away, in fact they will probably get worse and more of them will fall into our path. We cannot be sitting on the sidelines. Time is the greatest asset we have. What you decide to do with it is up to you. You now know the problems, take the necessary action that you see fit for your particular situation.

Inflation and its Effects on Purchasing Power

Have you ever gone to a store and wanted an item that is the newest latest and greatest? Maybe that item happens to be a new laptop computer. Let's say after a period of saving, you finally decide to go to the store and buy the laptop of your dreams. Upon arrival, and to your dismay, you find that the maker of the laptop has only seven of this particular laptop to sell and a waiting list of fifteen other people who also have their minds set on buying the same laptop. The store is now in a unique position of being able to charge a premium for the new laptops because the demand is so great. So the money you saved is not going to go quite so far as you thought it might. Such is the problem with inflation.

The purchasing power of your money is diminishing as the prices are rising. Consequently you will need more money to buy the things you really want. In early 2008, American consumers saw inflation eat into their wallets with the vast escalating rise in both food and energy commodities, which in turn resulted in much higher food and fuel costs. Food was reported to have risen as much as 20% since the same time a year earlier. There is an index that measures how inflation affects the average consumer known as the Consumer Price Index (CPI). The CPI tracks the change in price on a basket of goods and services over time. This "basket" is made up of things such as food, clothing, housing, recreation, health care, education, and transportation.

Since we have been tracking inflation it has averaged roughly 3.5%. If we can safely assume that it will continue to rise at 3.5% per year, let's take a quick look at how our purchasing power will be affected twenty and thirty years from now. If twenty years from now you accumulate $250,000, at 3.5% inflation, that would be the equivalent of someone today having $122,000. If you want to have the same buying power of $250,000 in today's dollars (as of 2008) you would need to accumulate $497,000. Going even further out, if in thirty years you accumulate $250,000 at 3.5% inflation, that would be equivalent to someone today having $86,000. If you want to have the same buying power of $250,000 in today's dollars (as of 2008) you would need to accumulate $701,000. Wages and income are supposed to rise along with the rising standard costs of living, but that does not always happen each and every year. If someone is saving for retirement, it's very important thing to keep in mind inflation and its effects on our purchasing power. Inflation, it is a part of our economy and affects our lives. Prices might rise slowly one year and sharply the next. So, if that laptop of your dreams is not affordable to you right now, give it some time.

Ups and Downs

While saving for retirement, there will be ups and downs. It is not healthy for the economy and markets to always go up. While we may want that, in a perfect world it simply cannot happen. Markets and business cycles have to fluctuate up and down for our economy to function properly. It may sound strange, but please be aware that when you save and invest, you will see your account fluctuate up and down. It is important to realize this so that you don't panic or get worried when things are not going the way you planned.

You are investing for the long term; always think long term. If you have a long term time horizon (10 years or more) you should feel confident that even if the markets go down, it will come back.

When market decline, people's natural reaction is to panic and feel worried. As an advisor, I saw a lot of this and here is what I would say to clients to calm them down. "I feel your concern as to what is going on in the market place right now, but I would like to ask you three questions." I heard a successful public speaker and entrepreneur ask these questions.

"Question #1: True or False? Every time the stock market has gone down, it has come back? The answer is True."

"Question #2: True or False? Every time the stock market has gone down and come back, it has set new highs? Again, the answer is true."

"Question #3: Why do most people lose money in the stock market then? The answer is because they do not have a strong stomach to get through the times when things look terrible."

Peter Lynch, who was one of the world's most successful investors correctly pointed out that "investor success is determined by the stomach, not the head." What he meant by that was that if you have a long term time horizon and you take the emotion of "the moment" out of investing, history has shown us that you will be just fine. There have been many times where the markets have looked bleak and scary, but as savers, it is vital to be patient and stay the course. So the risk is that history will not repeat itself. The risk is that once the markets go down they will never come back.

A Financial Hurricane

It is my opinion that our generation is going to see a financial hurricane; sooner rather than later. This hurricane will destroy the weak links in its path and the only survivors will be those who plan for the storm. The "weak links" in this analogy are the middle class and poor as they are beginning to get hit harder and harder financially. Many of these "weak links" will consist of baby boomers. They will be hit hard because of their lack of knowledge of unwillingness to have prepared earlier in life.

I once read an article titled, "Retire Where Jobs are Plentiful." The article went on to talk about how baby boomers want to work in retirement to stay active. This may be true for those who like their job or can find work, but for most people they will work in retirement because they have to. They will work in retirement because they didn't plan early and often enough. An article such as this written to baby boomers, in the year that they are beginning to retire, is astonishing. Why didn't this article come out four decades earlier? Many in the baby boomer generation have to live with the fact that they will have to work in retirement.

Remember when I talked about the 40% of the baby boomer generation that has saved $25,000 or less? Do you think they will want to work in retirement just to stay active, or do you think they will work in retirement because they have to? The latter is probably true. Our generation can start saving early and it doesn't have to be this way.

The Bureau of Labor Statistics reports that employees aged 50 or over now make up 28% of the U.S. workforce and that, by 2016, that proportion will rise to 33.5%, or more than one in three. According to a recent AARP survey, 8 out of 10 baby boomers want to keep working after they "retire". People have to go back to work in retirement because they say they still want to be challenged? I find it hard to believe that a job at Wal-Mart, greeting people and running the register at Target is what they had in mind as a way of being challenged? People will go back to work in "retirement" because they have to because they didn't plan for retirement early enough. They didn't have the education or knowledge or the foresight to see into the future and plan accordingly.

A study done by Northwestern Mutual shows: 85% of those people who set financial goals are happy vs. 53% of those people who do not set goals are happy. The study also asked, are you taking steps to achieve your goals? The survey shows that 89% that said yes say they have a high quality of life vs. 39% who said no.

A hurricane is very unpredictable. It can be weak or powerful, show mercy or be destructive. Hurricanes can change course at any given time leaving unprepared people vulnerable. The markets, economy and business cycles are the exact same way. Your retirement accounts can swing up and down violently just like a hurricane's winds can rise and fall. After a hurricane makes landfall, we look back at the destruction that took place and we wonder, why me?

When writing this book I lived in Southwest Florida, where hurricanes threaten our coast every year, and I know of the destruction and inconsistency of them more than most. Our generation is looking straight down the throat of a huge hurricane and as of right now, little is being done to prepare our generation for it. No one is working hard towards getting the "emergency supplies" that our generation needs. No one is out there talking and educating our generation how to prepare and beat this hurricane. No one is telling us that we need to make changes or this financial hurricane will crush us. The financial hurricane is coming. It has been sitting out there for decades gaining momentum, getting stronger and more destructive.

The problem with this financial hurricane is two fold. First, no one is out there diligently trying to educate our generation as to why or how it is coming. Secondly, no one is giving advice and direction to our generation on how to plan for it. How do you even prepare for a financial hurricane like this? What does it mean for me? How did this financial hurricane develop and what will its effects be?

Every time our government borrows more money, the financial hurricane strengthens. Just like a natural hurricane is so unpredictable, this financial hurricane is too. I don't know when it will strike us, but when it does it could be catastrophic. How will you be prepared for it? Don't be the one who is looking back after the hurricane comes through and say, "Wow, I should have better prepared."

How did the financial hurricane develop? This financial hurricane has been developing for years, even decades. You could trace the problem all the way back to the 1930's and the beginning of Social Security. Social Security was a program that was effective and worked in the 1930's. Going forward, Social Security is a flawed system and will need to be fixed. Part of this financial hurricanes power will stem from what will need to be done to fix the Social Security system by raising taxes, lowering benefits and waiting longer until we can receive benefits. These changes will need to be done in order to fix the system to function properly in today's day and age. Name me something that was started in the 1930's and still functions perfectly today, without any modifications or changes from its original form?

Another contributing factor to the hurricane is the fact that our economy is now a global one. The global economy has been evolving for years. As I write this, the European markets were down roughly 6% yesterday on worries of a bailout in the

European financial markets. Subsequently today the US markets sold off nearly 5% based solely on this European news. If that is not a global market, than I don't know what is. Never before has a generation had to worry about their investments being affected by what markets overseas are doing. Our generation and future generations, from the very beginning of our saving days, have that reality.

How much momentum this financial hurricane will have when it truly hits us is yet to be seen. What we as a generation can do is plan for it. How do you prepare for the financial hurricane? If you know a hurricane is coming, wouldn't you prepare for it? You get ready by buying emergency supplies, boarding up windows and if necessary leaving town for a few days. With the financial hurricane that is on the way, we as a generation need to plan as well. Instead of buying batteries, water and generators we need other supplies. We need supplies such as Roth 401(k)'s or 403(b)'s, Roth IRA's and emergency living funds. Instead of leaving town, we need to become educated and knowledgeable. We need to know that our retirement account can accumulate dramatically faster by starting earlier and we need to know the benefits each of our retirement accounts possesses. We need to know how dollar cost averaging works in our favor. It is one thing to read and learn about what to do, but it is another to actually go through with it. Action needs to be taken.

Think about a time when you had to make a change. It might have been when you had to change sports teams or change schools because your parents moved to a new town. As this financial hurricane approaches our generation, we need to make a change. Making change is never easy; sacrifices need to be made and lifestyles could be altered. I once had a client in my office that realized he needed to change the amount of hours he worked just to be able to contribute to his Roth IRA. The way he had it set up, he was not going to be able to contribute as much as he wanted, because of the income he was making. We talked about it, and he decided to make the change to work more hours and in turn was able to contribute what he wanted to his Roth IRA. He made sacrifices and made the change. As we begin our careers we need to makes changes.

One of our biggest responsibilities is setting up, contributing to and maintaining our retirement accounts. The problem is that no one teaches us this in school and many people fail to start at an early age. Our generation is handicapped by not being informed of our options and consequently we don't save nearly enough for retirement.

Paying Higher Taxes

Paying taxes is one of the few certainties in life. We all must pay taxes, wither it is income tax, social security tax, property tax, capital gains tax or tax on a Traditional IRA distribution, the government will get their tax dollars. One of the changes that this financial hurricane could bring about is higher taxes. If we have to pay higher taxes, that means less money in our pocket for our hard work and time put in. Below is a chart of the highest marginal tax rates going back to 1913.

13-Mar-07

Historical Highest Marginal Income Tax Rates

Year	Top Marginal Rate	Year	Top Marginal Rate	Year	Top Marginal Rate
1913	7.0%	1945	94.00%	1977	70.00%
1914	7.0%	1946	86.45%	1978	70.00%
1915	7.0%	1947	86.45%	1979	70.00%
1916	15.0%	1948	82.13%	1980	70.00%
1917	67.0%	1949	82.13%	1981	69.13%
1918	77.0%	1950	91.00%	1982	50.00%
1919	73.0%	1951	91.00%	1983	50.00%
1920	73.0%	1952	92.00%	1984	50.00%
1921	73.0%	1953	92.00%	1985	50.00%
1922	56.0%	1954	91.00%	1986	50.00%
1923	56.0%	1955	91.00%	1987	38.50%
1924	46.0%	1956	91.00%	1988	28.00%
1925	25.0%	1957	91.00%	1989	28.00%
1926	25.0%	1958	91.00%	1990	31.00%
1927	25.0%	1959	91.00%	1991	31.00%
1928	25.0%	1960	91.00%	1992	31.00%
1929	24.0%	1961	91.00%	1993	39.60%
1930	25.0%	1962	91.00%	1994	39.60%
1931	25.0%	1963	91.00%	1995	39.60%
1932	63.0%	1964	77.00%	1996	39.60%
1933	63.0%	1965	70.00%	1997	39.60%
1934	63.0%	1966	70.00%	1998	39.60%
1935	63.0%	1967	70.00%	1999	39.60%
1936	79.0%	1968	75.25%	2000	39.60%
1937	79.0%	1969	77.00%	2001	38.60%
1938	79.0%	1970	71.75%	2002	38.60%
1939	79.0%	1971	70.00%	2003	35.00%
1940	81.10%	1972	70.00%	2004	35.00%
1941	81.00%	1973	70.00%	2005	35.00%
1942	88.00%	1974	70.00%	2006	35.00%
1943	88.00%	1975	70.00%	2007	35.00%
1944	94.00%	1976	70.00%		

Note: This table contains a number of simplifications and ignores a number of factors, such as a maximum tax on earned income of 50 percent when the top rate was 70 percent and the current increase in rates due to income-related reductions in value of itemized deductions. Perhaps most importantly, it ignores the large increase in percentage of returns that were subject to this top rate.

Sources: Eugene Steuerle, The Urban Institute; Joseph Pechman, Federal Tax Policy; Joint Committee on Taxation, Summary of Conference Agreement on the Jobs and Growth Tax Relief Reconciliation Act of 2003, JCX-54-03, May 22, 2003; IRS Revised Tax Rate Schedules

My first question would be, "what are the lowest and highest marginal tax brackets going to be when you turn 60? The answer is, "We don't know." What we do know is that as of 2007, the highest marginal tax bracket was low compared to historical figures. 2007 saw a somewhat favorable highest marginal tax bracket. When our generation turns 60, the tax bracket could be 5% or it could be 90%. Take a look at the years from 1932-1981 where the highest marginal tax bracket never got below 63%. In the 1940's and 1950's it even got up as high as 94%. So it would not be far fetched to say that when we turn 60, the highest marginal tax brackets could be in the eighty or ninetieth percentile. Paying higher taxes is always a possibility.

What does this mean for your retirement accounts? If you know about the rules of the Roth 401(k) and the Roth IRA (which will be described later in this book) you would know that all qualified distributions from those accounts are tax free, so we don't care what the highest marginal tax bracket is when we retire. It could be 94% and for every $1 that you pull out of your Roth IRA (as long as it is a qualified withdrawal) you get $1. The IRS is allowing you (providing you contributed to a Roth IRA and the withdrawals are qualified) to take a distribution and pay $0 in taxes.

Assume that Bob and Ryan are best friends. Bob, has a Roth IRA and continually contributed to it each month. Ryan, has a regular 401(k) (not a Roth 401(k)) through his employer and continually contributed to it each month. The ending value they have is exactly the same, $1,000,000, upon reaching the age of 65, when they both decide to retire and begin taking distributions from their accounts. Bob can pull out his entire $1,000,000 income tax free. Ryan must pay taxes at the tax rates that are in place at that time. Knowing these advantages early enough in life, allows you to take action on the strategy and prepare for it. The longer you wait, the more you are losing out on and hurting yourself.

It is your retirement, how are you going to plan for it? This is a serious question and unfortunately it is not a question that the school system asks us before we get into the real world. I often wonder why the school system does not teach us this. I also often wonder why the only training employer's give is a packet in the mail telling me to call the 800 number if I have any questions. If no one teaches me what an IRA or a Roth 401(k) or a regular 401(k) or a 403(b) is, how do I know what questions to ask? Most people just go by what they hear others are doing. Bob will probably do the same thing Ryan is doing just because Ryan told him what he was doing. Bob will not do his own research because it's boring and takes too much time. The problem is that Bob and Ryan's situation may be completely different. I just find it hard to believe that no one is teaching our generation these important concepts and allowing us to be equipped with the proper information and tools to make an educated decision on one of the most important things in our lives, our retirement.

There will always be many unknowns. Will our taxes increase? How much will our taxes increase? Where will marginal tax rates be when I retire? Paying taxes is a given, but what tax we pay and when they change is the factor that we don't know. Do not be surprised if taxes fluctuate during your working and retirement years, they most likely will. Have the knowledge to know that accounts can legally be set up to combat high marginal tax rates. Since we don't get to make the legislation that tells us the taxes we must pay, take advantage of the legislation that allows us to set up an account to not pay taxes when it comes time for a distribution, an account such as the Roth IRA and a Roth 401(k).

Misconceptions

Have you ever though, "I wish I could invest and save but I just don't have the money to" or "I'll wait until later to start investing." These two thoughts are embedded in the minds of our generation. It is these two concepts that fuel the problem of our generation not being on track to save enough. My question to you would be, "Can you afford to save $50 a month? If you can, then you can start saving. If you can't, then my next question would be, "what would it take for you to be able to save $50 a month?"

The following is a list of ten misconceptions about saving for retirement that is quite common amongst our generation. They are comprised of reasons why people of our generation don't want to save and then reasons why they can or should.

Misconception #1:
You need a lot of money to start saving and investing.

This is the single biggest misunderstanding of people in our generation. Many people think that because they don't have $10,000 or $20,000 they can't start saving or investing. Saving is a process that takes time and discipline. As a financial advisor I signed up countless clients (in our generation) with as little as $100 initial investment and a contribution of $50 thereafter. If you can afford to save $50, you can start saving. There is a big difference between $10,000 and $50 as a monetary value, however saving, no matter what the amount, is huge. You do not need a lot of money to start saving and investing.

I commonly hear, "I don't make enough money to begin saving."

Saving $50 a month is equivalent to saving $1.66 a day. What in your daily routine accounts for $1.66 that can be eliminated? Start small with $30 or $50 a month, because saving something is always better than saving nothing.

Misconception #2:
You need a big income to accumulate a lot of wealth.

A large income does not necessarily translate into great wealth or prudent saving patterns. If you make a moderate income you will simply need to live below your means. Buy what you can afford and avoid the loose spending. I had clients who make $30,000 a year and are setting aside more money than someone making $100,000 a year. In my opinion the person making $30,000 a year is better off than the person making $100,000. A lot of people are prone to spend more when they make more. They are not necessarily more prone to save more as they make more. You do not need a big income to accumulate wealth.

Misconception #3:
You're Too Young To Start Saving

It is never too early to start saving. I wish my parents started saving for me when I was first born or made me save when I got my first job. They didn't and that is okay, but it would have been a great start. Think about that grass cutting job or part time work at the restaurant. That money can be set aside. There is no age requirement to start saving. It is difficult to think about saving when you have other things on your mind, such as school, athletics and extra curricular activities. Just because you are a teenager or in your early twenties, doesn't mean you can't begin to save. An 18 year old who invests $100 a month and earns 10% per year would accumulate $1,100,000 by age 65. If that person waited until age 28 (which is still earlier than the average American begins saving) he would accumulate $436,000 a difference of $664,000. Knowing this information now, may entice you to want to start saving at an early age. I'm sure we all wish we would have started at 18. Remember, you are never too young to start saving.

Misconception #4:
A Million Dollars Will Be Enough

It is my opinion that in 2047, the year I will turn 65, $1 Million will not be enough to fund an adequate retirement. Since we have been tracking it, inflation has averaged about 3.5%. If we can safely assume that it will continue to increase at 3.5% then what will our money buy us in the future? Twenty years from now, $250,000 will be like someone in 2008 having $122,000. Thirty years from 2008 someone with $250,000 will be the same as someone having $86,000 in 2008. We cannot forget about inflation and its effects on our purchasing power, it is here to stay.

Adjusting for annual 3.5% inflation one would need to save $3,825,371.71 to equate to $1,000,000 in 2008 terms. This means that to have the same buying power in 2047 as someone today having $1,000,000 you will need over $3,800,000. For our generation, $3.8 million is the new $1,000,000. Understand that wages, income, and contribution amounts will go up as the years go on. Also understand that we need to begin to realize that just accumulating $1,000,000 will not be enough for most to live off of. Accumulating $1,000,000 by age 65 would be like someone today having $249,209. Furthermore, $100,000 in today's dollars will be $382,537.17 in 2047. I use the general rule that in order to sustain longevity in your portfolio, withdrawal no more that 6% of the value of your account per year in distributions. If you do accumulate $1,000,000 by 2047 and are taking a 6% withdrawal rate to live off of, you will only be pulling off $60,000, which in 2047 terms would be like $14,952 in today's dollars. So if you can picture yourself living off of $14,952 a year or $1,246 a month, than $1,000,000 might be enough. More simply put, $1 Million will not be enough.

Misconception #5:
We Have No Control

Many people think that because they do not know much about saving or investing that they have no control. This is not true. You can have all the control you want. It depends on how involved you want to be. Investing in a lifecycle fund would give you control, since those funds automatically reallocates your account for you. Working with a professional advisor who watches over and manages your account is another way. The reason most people lose money in the markets, by their own, is because they save and invest on emotion and fear. Fear and uncertainty are things you can't predict. Risk, on the other hand, you can somewhat evaluate and predict. Evaluating and predicting risk allows you to formulate a risk tolerance, which in turn allows you to find an investment that is suitable. But again, the control can be all yours if you choose.

Misconception #6:
Saving and Investing are Too Complex

I will concede the fact that there are more investment options in the world today than what is really necessary. At the brokerage firm I worked for, we offered more than 16,000 mutual funds. I understand that when starting out in investing, you can be overwhelmed with all your options, making it seem like you are drinking out of a fire hydrant.

Here is a tip, if you want the most basic diversification and direction, select a lifecycle fund. Life cycle funds automatically rebalance to the proper allocation for you. Choose a life cycle fund that most accurately represents your retirement year (i.e. 2050) and the fund will do all the work for you. You don't have to do anything, monitor anything, make and investment decisions. All you have to do is contribute and wait until you reach your retirement age. Other resources are available to you, such as financialyoung.com where you can find very helpful information.

It is important to remember that past performance is not indicative of future returns. If you work with a professional, choose someone you trust. They should be able to guide you through all of the garbage that is out there. Investing and saving can be as simple as you want it to be.

Misconception #7:
I Can Withdrawal Money at Any Time

It is wrong to say that you can withdrawal money at any time out of your employer sponsored plan or IRA accounts. Each account has its own set of rules as to when a withdrawal can be taken out. In some cases, if a premature distribution is taken, both a penalty and or a taxable event could occur. As of the time of this writing, a withdrawal can be taken after the age of 59 ½. There currently are some exceptions as to when a withdrawal can be taken prior to the age of 59 ½. These exceptions are subject to change, but currently are considered a qualified distribution. Accounts such as 401(k)'s and IRA's are not designed for you to contribute to them for one year and then withdrawal the money. If you do so, it could be considered a qualified distribution and you may be penalized and taxed.

These accounts are designed for you to accumulate money for retirement and therefore have an age barrier at which you must obtain, not including the exceptions, with which you can take out money with no penalty. For a list of the current years withdrawal limits visit financialyoung.com. But remember you can not withdrawal money from your qualified accounts at "any time" without meeting certain criteria.

Misconception #8:
Missing a Year of Contributions Will Not Hurt Me Much

This may be the biggest misconception of our generation. The key to growing your accounts is more about the amount of time that you save and not the amount of money. Missing just one year of contributions can drastically reduce your savings in the long run and let me show you how that is.

Let's assume that at age 25, Saver A makes an initial contribution in his retirement account of $250 and contributes $100 a month for the next forty years earning an average annual return of 12%. At age 65, Saver A has accumulated

$1,054,233.61. Saver B starts saving one year after Saver A, and when he starts he does all the same things Saver A did. He invested $250 initially, contributed $100 a month into the same fund, but because Saver B missed that first year, he only received an average annual return 11.5% Saver B accumulated $817,664.08. That is a difference of $236,569. Both savers are now age 65, and because Saver A started just one year earlier, he has accumulated $236,569 more than Saver B. When showing this example, people are shocked that Saver A has accumulated so much more. You potentially are missing out on a lot when waiting just one year to start saving and investing.

Misconception #9:
It's Okay I don't Invest Now, I'll Play Catch Up

Playing catch up is one of the hardest things to do. We get into our habits and they are hard to break. Even as we begin to make more money, we tend to spend that money, not save it. If we use the example from the previous misconception, since Saver B started one year after Saver A, he would need to invest roughly $125 a month over that same time span just to break even with Saver A's account value at age 65. Over the course of that twenty year time span, Saver B would need to contribute $11,700 more out of his own pocket just because he started one year later.

If we use the average American, who begins saving at age 40, he would need to set aside $7,500 a year or $625 a month to get where Saver A is at age 65. If we look at a breakdown of total out of pocket contributions, Saver A has contributed $48,000 over the course of the forty years. This average American has contributed $187,500 over the course of twenty-five years; a difference of $139,500 in total out of pocket contributions between the two savers. The longer you procrastinate on saving and investing, the harder it is to play catch up.

If you are planning on waiting to save for your future, now may be the time to reconsider. Think about setting aside money each month and getting rid of the notion that "It's okay that you don't save now, you will play catch up" because playing catch up is very hard.

Misconception #10:
We Can Live the Same Way as Our Parents

The theme of this book is that the times have changed and we need to change too. The best way I can explain this is by saying that we will not have the luxury of living the way our parents have lived. The days of multiple homes, multiple cars and free running credit, I am afraid, are most likely behind us. We as a younger generation see our parents and our friend's parents live with nice things, luxuries and toys and we just assume or expect that that will be our reality too. Well since the times have changed, we need to change.

Our parents have lived through a market that has been very good to them. Easy credit and free flow spending has been too loose for too long and our economy is now seeing the effects of it. Even our own government has been on a giant spending spree and accumulated trillions in debt that needs to be paid back. Who is going to pay back that debt that the government has piled up? My guess is that it will be our generation. How long can our debt continue to stock pile before something needs to be done? We will have to fix the mounting debt our country has accumulated. This is debt that our grandparents and our parents' generation have accumulated through the years.

The burden of paying it back these large debts could fall on our generation. Drastic measures may need to be taken in order to get our debt back in line that is sustainable. Only time will tell how this will all play out, but my generation will not have the same luxuries that previous generations have had.

The New Middle Class

2008 was a tough year. There had been many issues the country has faced. Going forward, there will be a new face of the middle class. It brings attention to the fore front for a couple reasons. As the cost of everyday consumer goods such as fuel and food shoot up dramatically, many middleclass Americas find themselves having to sacrifice little luxuries in life. It get's to a point for many where they have to decide between going on vacation or filling up the gas tank for the month. I am not an economist, but I am a realist and I see many examples of middleclass people struggling and I see little end to this in the foreseeable future.

The middleclass is getting pinched out of this country and we will be left with two types of people, rich and lower class. This phenomenon will be our reality for some time. Everything goes in cycles, but many experts are considering this the worst economic times since the great depression. We are young and many opportunities are out there for the taking. One of the greatest declines in stocks is happening right now, which means there is potential for one of the greatest run up on stocks in the foreseeable future. For now, the middle class will struggle and become the new lower class. I would recommend that you work hard to be able to save money each month. Things will be tight, but you will thank yourself later in life, I promise.

Part 3

What Can I Do?

Start Saving Now

Our generation needs to start saving now. It does not matter if you save $1,000 or $50 a month. We have seen examples of how small contributions over the long term add up. The one thing that we now know is that the longer you save and invest, the better off you can be. So if you know this, why wouldn't you do everything you can to start saving? The times have changed and we need to change too.

Being in the financial advisory business, I can personally tell you of the many stories and times I have heard my own clients state they wish they had saved more. They wish they had begun saving earlier in life. Once I tell them the things I am telling you today, their only response is, "that is so smart" and "I wish someone told me to do this when I was your age." They also say things like, "You have a smart head on your shoulders, you are lucky." I did not invent the idea of saving or investing for retirement, but I do know how to take advantage of the rules that are in place. The advantages of saving and investing in an IRA and 401(k) through my employer and having six months of reserve funds saved up.

Knowing that the times have changed and we may not be able to depend on Social Security, Medicare and company pensions is good to know now rather than later. If these problems continue as they are, we will not be able to depend on these things, and this has not been experienced by any other generation.

I once saw a program on TV where a couple in their mid forties were getting interviewed by a talk show host. The show was centered on people who spend too much and don't save enough. As I watched this couple spill their guts about their lavish spending habits, I began to think about how they would have loved to of read this book back in their twenties. I know this because of the tears coming down their cheeks as they described what trouble they got themselves into. They were in their mid forties with two children and almost $100,000 in debt. This is not necessarily out of the norm in today's day and age, but they had got into debt by buying foolish things such as tools that had not even been taken out of the package, vacations and cars that they couldn't afford. I watched for ten minutes as this couple poured their heart out in front of the country on this nationally televised show. It must have been hard for them to come to the realization that they had messed up big time.

A finance consultant was working with this couple and told them that had they started saving in their twenties they would have already accumulated a substantial amount of money. The finance consultant told them that in order to break even, to where they want to be when they turn 65, that they now need to save $4,200 a month. When the couple heard this news, the tears began to flow out again. They knew there was no way they could save $4,200 a month. The realization that they needed to drastically change their lifestyle was happening in front of the entire country. I have to imagine that there are thousands, if not millions of others in this country that are in a similar situation as this couple.

The reason the average American begins saving for retirement in their forties is because they don't have the knowledge to start saving small amounts early on in life and as their income grows, save more. People don't want to live within their means because they see their next door neighbor buy a new boat or car, or toy. People feel inferior if they do not have all the things that their friends and neighbors have. Let's assume that this couple that we have just spoken of started saving $100 a month from the age of 20. Each year we will adjust their contribution up 2.7% to adjust for inflation and increase in wages. If they earn 8% per year on their investment, by the time they turn 65 they would have accumulated $532,000. If they think that will not be enough then they will have to find a way to save more per month.

Let's compare that outcome to another couple doing the same thing, but starting at 45. By the time they turn 65 they would accumulate $63,968, which is a difference of $459,000. In order to have just as much (in this example) starting at 45, this couple would need to save $ $875 a month instead of $100. The difference is huge. It is for this reason right here that you need to start saving right now.

If time and time again you hear that making small contributions, earlier in life and over the long run add up to more as opposed to waiting (all other things being equal) then why would you not start saving right now? That is a question you need to answer. The tools and resources are right at your fingertips for your exposure. Great things can happen with a little education and some action. Opening up a Roth IRA is a huge step towards securing one of the most important aspects of your life, retirement.

How to Get Started

Okay, now you are all pumped up, motivated and ready to take on the world. So how do you get started? The very first step in getting started is actually believing that the times are changing and that you need to change along with them. If you don't believe this, then you are probably not going to make the necessary changes to achieve what you want financially. Building wealth is all about the time you put in. Once we lose today we can never get it back. Trying to convince someone my age to buy into the theory of setting money aside for retirement right now, is one of the hardest things I have ever done. No one wants to listen, change their habits and no one thinks it is important right now, because they don't see that the world has changed. So the very first step in getting started is convincing yourself that change is imminent and that we as a generation need to change too. Once you believe, you have left the starting blocks and are on your way.

The next important factor is getting educated and knowledgeable on the subject at hand. With all the resources and investments available, saving and planning can be a tricky complex subject. Go to www.financialyoung.com, which is a site devoted to the younger generation and is a wealth of knowledge. I would encourage you to also seek out advice from people you trust such as family, friends and relatives.

If you are convinced that change is happening and that we as a generation need to change, then you need to put together an action plan. For reference purposes, there is a sample in the back of this book. Keep your action plan somewhere you will always see it. Try hard to follow the action plan, and do not make it so hard that it is impossible to follow.

Lastly, I would recommend, providing you qualify, that you open up and contribute to a Roth IRA and/or a Roth 401(k). The Roth IRA will be discussed in great detail in this book and is a must have for everyone in our generation (providing you qualify). As of 2008, it is estimated by Fidelity Investments that 90% of American households are eligible for a Roth IRA, yet only 19% actually contribute to one. The benefits it brings cannot be achieved in any other investment vehicle. The initial limits are low enough now, where even a high school student with a part time job can contribute to one. Once a Roth IRA is set up, they can be extremely flexible towards your needs, wants and goals. It is important to remember that even though it may not seem like you are saving a lot (if you are saving $50 a month) you need to see the big picture that down the road you will be so much better off.

It Won't Happen Overnight

Maybe you have already read books on how to become rich quickly in the stock market using detection software. The likely hood of achieving overnight success and sustaining it are very slim. Think about what you can invest in; real estate, an allocation of mutual funds, bonds, these are long term investment and savings vehicles. Sure you can get into some speculative investments, and only a fraction of those investments actually work out. My point here is that to diligently accumulate money, you need time on your side.

Start to think about the accumulation phase of your life as making constant and consistent contributions over a long period of time. The longer you contribute, the more you can potentially accumulate. The following is an example that portrays what I am mean. Let's assume that the week after you are born your parents decided to put $100 a month into a savings vehicle for you that would generate 10% return on investment per year. By the time you turn 18 that account would grow to $49,000. Furthermore, upon turning 18 your parents say, "Okay that is enough," and they stop their $100 a month contribution; you could still allow that money to grow for you. If that money continues to grow at the same 10% per year, by the time you turn 60 you would accumulate $1,600,000. The longer you contribute, the more you can accumulate.

I like to ask people, "wouldn't you want to get started on something like this as soon as possible?" If your parents waited five years to begin this $100 a month contribution and started it when you were 5, by the time you turned 18 you would accumulate $28,000. Again, assuming that at the time you turned 18 your parents stopped all contributions and you let the money continue to grow at 10% per year, you would still accumulate $1,100,000 by the time you turned 60. The reason these accounts grow so much is because of compounding interest. The more you accumulate the more the interest that you earn affects your portfolio, both in a positive and negative way.

Building an adequate nest egg is a race against time. If you want to be able to retire someday knowing you have enough to sustain the lifestyle you want to live, you must prepare earlier. Our generation and the generations to follow must think and act differently than any other generation before us. We must take action and we must realize that financially, we can get to where we want to be. We must realize what the problems are, what the solution is and then take action on it. Start thinking like this and you will have the potential to accumulate great things, not overnight, but in the long term.

The 5 Stages of Early Retirement Planning

This section of the book goes into five important steps in getting started on the right foot. Knowing what you're getting involved in and becoming educated on the history, the problems and the risks of a project beforehand is very important. I view retirement planning no differently. So as part of the 5 stages of early retirement planning, I feel it is necessary to become educated and know where we as a country are headed and some of the challenges we as a generation will face.

Stage #1: Learn the History

Stage one is an ongoing stage. There is too much history of the markets and coupled with that they are always changing. Drastic changes are being made. But here is a brief and very vague history of the stock markets. As of 2007 the size of the equity (stock) market is roughly $60.9 Trillion. A stock market is one of the most important and efficient ways for companies to raise money for their business. When you purchase a share of stock such as Google, you are buying a share of ownership in the company. If you own a share of Google stock, you are an owner of the company. Your liability as an owner in that company is only to the extent to what you invested. If you invested $1,000 into Google stock you are only liable for that $1,000 even if the company goes bankrupt. If the company does go bankrupt your stock will become worthless and you will lose your entire investment. Companies continually offer new shares in an effort to raise money for their business operations. In return for you buying a share, they are giving you an ownership interest in the company. That is why a company that trades on a stock exchange is called a publicly traded company. Just like anything else, whenever there is a seller of a share of stock, on the other end there is a buyer.

Since the Dow Jones Industrial Average opened in the late 1890's, investors have seen positive growth over the long term. The DJIA is just one of many indexes that investors use as a gauge for how the overall economy is doing. Some say that the market is a predictor of what is to come maybe 6-12 months from now. The DJIA, as it is today, is only made up of 30 companies, which is not a very well diversified barometer to use. The companies that make up the DJIA can be removed and added at any time. The longest running company in the DJIA is General Electric (GE), which was added to the DJIA in 1907.

A better benchmark to use when looking at the overall equity market in the US is the S&P 500. This is an index that is made up of the 500 largest US companies. The S&P 500 can be altered at any time and often is. Companies go into and out of the index based on their market size. Typically speaking a company must have $4 Billion in market capitalization to be included in the S&P index. Using an index of 500 companies as opposed to 30, is a much better reference as to what is going on in the overall market, which is why most experts use the S&P 500 as the benchmark.

There is a term that is used frequently in the markets and that term is volatility. Volatility is a measure of how stocks are being bought and sold. The more stocks being bought and sold the higher the volatility will be. Vice versa, the less stocks are being bought and sold the lower the volatility will be. Saying that volatility will fluctuate during the course of time is a given. We as investors need to look at history and see this. We also need to know that past results are not an indication of what will happen in the future. Now you have a brief and vague history of the equity markets, as they are today. The markets are always changing and if you are interested, you can research them more. But as you begin to save for retirement, at the very least, you now know a little history of the stock markets.

Stage #2: Get Educated

Getting educated in how to plan and prepare for retirement planning is one of the most important things you will ever learn. It is the second stage in the early retirement planning process and probably the most important of all the five stages. Now that you have a little knowledge of the history, you can begin to learn what is available to you and how to go about getting involved. There are many ways you can go about getting the education you need, but for the beginner, it is important that you start with the basics and then move your way up. You can learn the basics by going to www.financialyoung.com under the Investor Education Tab. This will provide you with a wealth of information that will always be updated to meet the changing times.

You need to be aware of the alarming statistics of past generations and their saving habits. We can learn from them and do things differently. You need to learn how the times have changed and why we need to change as well. The earlier you can learn the concepts of beginning to save, the better off you can be later in life. Why is it that we go through twelve years of school and then possibly another four years in college and graduate schooling and the closest we ever come to learning about saving for retirement is maybe a class on the stock market? In my opinion our school system is flawed and it needs to be fixed. How can something so important, such as knowing how to start saving for retirement, not be taught in our schooling systems? The only way to learn about these topics is to do your own research, learn from a friend or family member, or read some literature your employer may give you on their employer sponsored plan.

If you are not interested in learning about retirement planning at an early age, you are not alone. Most of us are not interested at this age, and the only reason I was intrigued at an early age is because of my own research and the fact that I went into this profession right out of college. Had it not been for this reason I would not have started saving. Many people who are into their thirties have not yet done a thing to save for retirement. They are not doomed, yet they have a lot of catching up to do. They need to become educated on the importance of saving and why and how things are changing.

If you know you can accumulate more, by starting earlier in life and you also know it does not take a lot of money to contribute each month, why wouldn't you do it? If you listened to the baby boomer generation tell their story as to why they have not saved enough, and how they wish they could go back in time and do it differently, wouldn't you want to listen to that message? The reason they did not save enough is because they didn't have the education to know to start early in life. As a financial advisor I saw it everyday. Everyday I would hear a new person say, "I wish I had saved more when I was younger."

I often get asked the question, "Do you save for retirement?"

I answer with a resounding "Yes".

Their next question is always, "How old are you?"

I answer, "I am 25 years old."

Then they usually finish the conversation with, "I wish I would have done what you're doing." All it took was a little education which turned into motivation which turned into making a few sacrifices which turned into me taking action. That's all it will take for you too.

Stage #3 Realize the Problems Our Generation Will Face

This stage is a vital step in the early stages of retirement planning. Our generation, like all generations, will face challenges as we grow older. Our saving and investing demeanor will change. The thing that is different from past generations to ours is that we can't afford to wait; we must act early and often. We are looking straight down the barrel of a generational shotgun and we need to get out of the way. The only way to avoid getting caught in the crossfire is that you know it's coming.

Listed are just a few of the problems, and I mean huge problems I see our generation having to overcome. Social Security, lack of company pensions, longevity of life and medical costs. Our generation, more so than any other, will face these problems head on. Our generation will be so much more affected because, the systems are flawed, they are running out of money and we will live longer, leaving us to deal with the problems for longer. Our generation has to begin to see this and take action.

Many people say, "if it's not broke, don't fix it." Well a lot of our systems are broke and they need fixing. The sad truth is that no one is telling this to our generation. When something is broke it needs to be fixed, and the issues at hand here are broken. The Social Security system is running into the problem of having less people pay into the system each year. If this trend continues, we could eventually reach a point where more people are receiving benefits than are paying into the benefit pool. What type of problem do you think that would bring about? My guess is s huge one. Will we eventually get that deep? I highly doubt it, but the things that will need to be done to fix the problems will somewhat handcuff us.

Will my company give me a pension when I retire? I cannot say with any confidence that a company will continue to give out pensions for retirees. We live in a world now where companies can't afford it and if they can they probably will not continue to issue pensions. So if I have a reduced Social Security amount, no pension from my employer, I am living longer and my medical costs are going sky high, how am I ever going to retire? Well I am probably going to have to start planning and saving a lot sooner that what I thought. I am going to have to save before I even start my career. I am going to have to do things my entire career that will allow me to potentially retire one day. I will have to do things like save early and often, increase my contributions to keep up with inflation, set aside emergency funds and protect my family with the use of insurance.

These things are not drastically different than what is done today, in fact they are the are things people do today, the difference is when you start. Today, the average American begins saving in their forties. I challenge you to realize that starting in your forties is way too late. I challenge you to begin in your twenties, if not earlier and be ahead of the curve. As long as you have income, there is no rule or law against saving. There are many saving vehicles out there for you to take advantage of, so start today and use those advantages to get ahead in life.

Stage #4 Begin Taking Action

This is one of the easiest steps, but for some reason, most people have a hard time actually starting. They convince themselves that starting to save is a good idea; they can see that change is taking place and that they need to change too, but for whatever reason they do not start. I usually hear people say, "I don't have a lot of money" or "Ill wait until later to start" or "ill play catch up later in life." There are a million reasons people don't start saving.

Setting up a savings vehicle literally takes about five minutes. After you are set up, everything can take place electronically, allowing you to view all activity online. I will give you an example of what I mean.

Bob opened up a Roth IRA at his local bank and it took him five minutes to fill out the forms, and once the forms were filled out and submitted, he was done. Bob had selected to contribute $200 on the 15th of each month. So on the same day every month Bob's $200 contribution comes out of his bank account and into the IRA. Bob does not have to write a check, or go to the bank because it is all done electronically, automatically, for free each month. Bob never has to think about making his contribution; it is so automatic and easy. If Bob ever wanted to contribute more or less or stop his contribution for whatever reason, he can.

After the initial setup your retirement account does all the work for you. In the previous example, Bob loves his automatic withdrawal because he is paying himself first. Right after Bob gets paid, he is contributing to his retirement account. There is no temptation of spending the money. Bob can't spend the money, since it goes directly into his retirement account the day after he gets paid. Again, you know you are going to have to save for retirement sometime. You know that all it takes to start is $50 a month. You also know that starting earlier rather than later, even if it is only $50 a month will give you the potential to accumulate so much more in the long run.

I would encourage you to take action. Use resources like financialyoung.com to become more educated on your options. Talk to your friends and family members. Don't go into something if you do not understand it. Take the time to learn, before you act. Please, take my advice on this. I have already lost everything and know the feeling of failure. It is worth researching and learning about before you get involved. It does not take much to learn about the basics, and once you do, it is so important to take action.

Stage #5 Spread the Word of Your Knowledge

My job now is to spread the word. I work hard every day to share my knowledge with my generation so that they may begin to realize that saving is important. This is a monumental task and I cannot do it alone. I need the help of every one of you to spread the word. I use this saying all the time, "If I can influence one person every day, I feel I have done my job." I truly believe in that, and it gives me a good feeling when I can spread this message and people receive it well. Once you have learned that the times are changing, try telling someone you know that would appreciate knowing this information as well. Tell them that there are resources available at their disposal. Refer them to your favorite educational hot spots. Tell them to look at what you have learned. Tell them success stories like how you opened up a Roth IRA and are now on your way to putting your retirement plans in your own hands. That is a powerful statement. "I have put my retirement plans in my own hands." You will not be dependent on someone else deciding when and if you can retire.

Think about how adults will look at you when you tell them you are saving in both a Roth IRA and a 401(k). I am telling you they will be impressed. But don't just do it to impress others, do it because you really want to. Do it because you understand that saving early in life is important. Some people could care less about saving and they will never believe that saving for retirement is necessary. They will float through life and that is their decision. Save and invest for all the right reasons. Save for reasons such as, you want to retire comfortably; and that you know the changes are coming and you want to prepare for them. You can help spread the word and in the end those people will be appreciative. I now feel I have an obligation to spread the message and I hope that you will take the liberty of helping me out and spread the message too.

Plan Now For the Unexpected

Things happen that cannot always be explained. Things happen that we never thought would. I learned this the hard way by losing everything, all my savings, my rental property and my primary residence by the age of 25. Planning for the unexpected is hard to do. Planning ahead is not hard to do, and that is how you combat the unexpected that might happen.

Here is an example of four people who all planned on retiring at 65, but had to unexpectedly retire at the age of 62. They lost three years of saving and compounding power due to the unexpected. Below is a chart of the difference in retirement account values. Each person invested $10,000 at the starting age given and the money grew at an annual average rate of 10%.

Starting Age	Value if you Retire at 65	Value if you Retire at 62	Difference
20	$ 728,904.00	$ 547,636.00	$ 181,268.00
30	$ 281,024.00	$ 221,137.00	$ 59,887.00
40	$ 108,347.00	$ 81,402.00	$ 26,945.00
50	$ 41,772.00	$ 31,384.00	$ 10,388.00

You can see why preparing early is so important. The saver that started at age 20 has lost out on a potential $181,268 in earnings due to an unexpected situation. He has still saved up a nice nest egg, but is still short of where he thought he would be. Maybe instead of just investing the $10,000 he originally invested, he could have set aside $100 a month. Over the course of that forty-two year span it would have grown into a nice chunk of money with which to use for retirement. Unexpected things happen all the time. Prepare for them early on and you will thank yourself for it. I got burned early in my life and now I have learned to plan for the unexpected. If it ever happens again, I will be ready. I encourage you to be ready as well.

Below are some statistics that you may not have been aware of. They are very interesting and I thought you might find them intriguing. The numbers are according to the Employee Benefit Research Institute (EBRI) 2008 Retirement Confidence Survey.

1. The percentage of people who believe they will have saved enough to have a comfortable retirement is 18%, down from 27%. In other words, 82% of people polled believe they will not have saved enough for retirement.
2. When asked what is the most pressing financial issue facing Americans today, only 5% of workers said saving or planning for retirement.
3. When asked where your retirement income will come from?

80% said from Social Security
74% said from an employer sponsored plan such as a 401(k) or 403(b)
73% said from other personal saving or investments
69% said from an IRA

4. When asked what is your method of determining savings needed for retirement?
    43% said they GUESS
    19% ask a financial advisor
    19% do their own estimate
    9% read or hear how much is needed
    7% use an online calculator
    4% fill out a worksheet or form

5. When asked the amount of savings American workers think they will need for retirement
    25% said < $250k
    16% said $250k-499k
    23% said 500k-999k
    11% said $1MM-$1.99MM
    7% said $2MM+
    12% have no clue

American workers are not saving enough and they know it and the problem is that they are running out of time. Our generation can fix this problem if we know that the problem exists. I ask the question, "If you don't know where you want to go, how in the world can you begin to get there?" You can't, it's impossible. That is why you need to learn at an early enough age about where you want to be by the time you retire. Don't become one of the percentages above. Don't let the days pass by where you take no action. Don't let a lack of planning leave you unprepared.

The IRA

An individual retirement account (IRA) is a tax-favored savings plan through which an individual saves for retirement. An IRA can benefit an individual through the tax-deferred or tax free compounding of earnings and a possible tax deduction for contributions. An IRA owner has the legal right to revoke any IRA for 7 days after the client receives the IRA disclosure statement and custodial agreement. These documents must be given no later than the day the client signs the IRA agreement. The date on the agreement starts the 7 day period. IRA contribution Limits: Annual IRA contributions cannot exceed the amount of compensation for the year or the annual contribution dollar amount, whichever is less. Compensation is generally what you earn from working.

An individual can contribute to an IRA for a non-working spouse even though the spouse has no compensation. Annual contributions for both spouses are limited to the combined annual contribution amounts for that year or 100% of earned income (of working spouse), whichever is less. Contributions are made to separate IRAs for each spouse. Individual annual contributions are limited to a maximum dollar amount per person per tax year for traditional and Roth IRAs combined. The annual contribution amount, per person, can be contributed to either type of IRA or divided between the two. The maximum annual contribution is as follows:

In 2008 and after $5,000 (indexed for inflation in $500 increments). If you are over the age of 50 you can make a $1,000 catch up contribution as well.

Deduction Limits: If the individual is not an active plan participant during the year (and, if married, spouse is also not an active plan participant) a traditional IRA contribution would be fully deductible. Roth IRA contributions are not tax deductible.

Deadlines: The deadlines for establishing and funding an IRA (traditional or Roth IRA) for an individual contribution is the due date of the individual's federal tax return not including extensions (generally April 15). If the deadline falls on a weekend or holiday, the deadline is the next business day.

3 Types of IRA's:

1. Standard/Traditional IRA: A person who has earned income (or receives alimony) can make an annual contribution to an IRA. The annual contribution cannot exceed the annual contribution limit or 100% of earned income, whichever is less. Contributions must be made by check or money order. The contributions may or may not be tax deductible. A traditional IRA contribution may be made up until the deadline (generally April 15), even after filing that year's tax return. Individual traditional IRA contributions are not allowed for the tax year in which you turn age 70 ½ , and beyond.

2. Rollover IRA: A rollover is a deposit of assets into an IRA by an individual who has received a distribution (of cash, stock or other assets) from another retirement plan. A rollover can result from prior distribution from another IRA or from an employer retirement plan. The purpose of the rollover is to defer the obligation to pay taxes on the distribution. A rollover is different than a transfer. An IRA coded as a rollover account will still accept the individuals personal contribution. In addition, an account not coded as a rollover will accept rollovers and direct rollover transfers.

3. Roth IRA (most likely what you will want to get): To make a Roth IRA contribution, you must have 1) earned income, and 2) MAGI below stated IRS limits. There is no deduction for a Roth contribution. A Roth IRA contribution may be made up until the deadline (generally April 15), even after filing that year's tax return. The earnings in a Roth IRA may be distributed income tax-free only after a 5-year holding period and one of the following:

1.   Attainment of age 59 1/2

2. Death
3. Disability
4. First time home purchase (limited to $10,000)
5. Certain medical expenses
6. Medical insurance premium while unemployed
7. Qualified higher education expenses
8. A series of substantially equal periodic payments

Annual Roth IRA contributions may be withdrawn at any time without penalty or tax. The Roth IRA allows for contributions beyond age 70 ½ if the individual has earned income. The Roth IRA does not require minimum distributions at 70 ½. Eligibility for a contribution is based on Modified adjusted gross Income (MAGI) limits which are indexed annually. A copy of 2008's contribution eligibility chart is in the back of this book.

Below is a little history of the IRA: Fidelity Investments estimates that 90% of American households are eligible for a Roth IRA, yet only 19% actually have one. Since Roth 401(k)'s came out in 2006, fewer than 10% of employees who have this choice at work contribute.

Effective Tax Year	
	IRAs were created by the Employee Retirement Income Security Act (ERISA) in 1974.
1975	IRAs were for individuals not covered by employer sponsored plans. Contribution limit was the lesser of $1,500 or 15% of compensation.
1976	Annual contribution limit raised to $1,750. Spousal IRAs began.
1979	Simplified Employee Pension Plans (SEPs) began.

1982	Regular IRA contributions increased to lesser of $2,000 or compensation. IRA eligibility expanded to include anyone with earned income under age 70 1/2.
1987	Limits were placed on deductibility for certain individuals covered by employer plans. Nondeductible IRAs began.
1993	Direct rollovers from qualified plans to IRAs are allowed
1997	Spousal IRA contribution limit increased to $2,000. Savings Incentive Match Plan for Employees (SIMPLE) IRAs began. Establishment of new Salary Reduction SEP (SAR-SEP) no longer allowed
1998	Roth IRAs and Education Savings Accounts (ESAs) were created. Conversion from traditional IRA to Roth allowed 4-year spread on taxes for 1998 conversions. Adjusted Gross Income (AGI) limits for IRA deductibility are raised. Separate deductibility rules apply for joint returns when one spouse is not covered by plan.
2001	Proposed changes to Required Minimum Distribution (RMD) rules make significant changes to 2001 RMD calculations - reduced RMD amounts for almost everyone.
2002	IRA contribution limits raised to $3,000. Final regulations on RMDs were issued.
2003	Application of final regulations on required minimum distributions (RMD) required.

2005	IRA contribution limits raised to $4,000. In determining eligibility for Roth conversion, IRA RMD's are disregarded when figuring $100,000 MAGI.
2006	IRA contribution Limits raised to $5,000 for those age 50 or older. Qualified Charitable Distributions available for traditional and Roth IRA owners who are over age 70 1/2.
2007	Direct rollovers from qualified plans into inherited IRAs (fbo IRAs) by non-spousal beneficiaries allowed. Availability to direct income tax refunds to IRAs for contributions. MAGI limits traditional IRA contribution deduction and Roth IRA contribution eligibility are adjusted for inflation.
2008	IRA contribution limits raised to $5,000 for those under age 50. IRA deduction MAGI limits and Roth IRA contribution MAGI limits adjusted for cost of living. Direct conversion from qualified plan to Roth, if eligible for conversion.

To recap, the IRA, particularly the Roth IRA is a must for anyone in our generation who qualifies. A Roth IRA allows a saver to take advantage of tax-deferral (you don't pay taxes every year on your gains) and allows you to make a qualified withdrawal tax free. These advantages are too good to pass up. In my humble opinion every person that qualifies for a Roth IRA should have one. If you are still uncertain as to if you qualify or not, ask yourself if you have earned income? If you do then you need to ask yourself how much income do I have? If you need more details, visit www.financialyoung.com .

Furthermore the Roth 401(k) was introduced in 2006. If your employer provides for one, I strongly encourage that you invest in it. The Roth 401(k) has the same features as the Roth IRA and if your employer gives you a percentage match then that is even better. If you invest in a Roth 401(k) and/or a Roth IRA, what you are doing is eliminating any taxes that need to be paid when you make a qualified withdrawal, providing the rules stay the way they are now (in 2008).

Think about this for a minute. Suppose that you accumulate $1,000,000 in each of your Roth IRA and Roth 401(k) by the age of 65. If tax law stays the same, you can pull out all $2,000,000 tax free no matter what the tax rates at that time. That is very powerful and to know this at an early age and contribute to it is a huge advantage.

Employer Sponsored Plan: 401(k), 403(b)

A 401(k) plan is an employer sponsored plan that allows an employee to save for retirement on a tax-deferred basis. Depending on the employers plan the employee may be eligible to take advantage of a match contribution by the employer. If this happens to be the case, I highly recommend you participate and take advantage of the "free money" the company gives you.

Here is a simple example of how it works. Let's assume that you work for company XYZ and you contribute to their 401(k) plan. You contribute 6% of your monthly paycheck to your 401(k) account. Assuming that you earn $4,000 a month that would mean you're before tax contribution would be $240. Since XYZ Corporation matches up to 6% of what you put in dollar for dollar, XYZ Corp. will put in $240 into your 401(k) as well just because you are participating. That $240 that XYZ contributes is free money to you. All contributions to a 401(k) plan are with pre-tax dollars. The account grows on a tax-deferred basis, meaning you don't pay taxes on the gains each year. In fact you don't pay taxes until you pull the money out and when you do, you are taxed at your ordinary income level.

You must wait until you are 59 ½ to take a distribution from your 401(k). If you take a distribution before that age you will be subject to a 10% penalty of whatever amount you pull out. For example, if you take a distribution at age 35 of $5,000 you will pay a 10% penalty of $500 along with tax at your ordinary income level.

At age 70½ the IRS forces you to begin taking withdrawals from your 401(k) account in what is called a required mandatory distribution (RMD). This is because you have not paid any tax on this money yet and at age 70½ the government wants their tax dollars, so they force you to begin withdrawals, thus making you pay taxes. There are a few exceptions that you can take a distribution from a 401(k) plan before the age of 59 ½ and not pay the 10% penalty. One thing is always certain, whenever you take a distribution from a 401(k) plan, you will pay taxes at your ordinary income level.

The reason for the 10% penalty on unqualified withdrawals before the age of 59 ½ is because the 401(k) account is designed for you to save for retirement. They are not designed for you to contribute to, possibly get a company match contribution and then take a distribution five years later. They were designed to allow the accounts to grow for retirement.

The annual limits for how much you can contribute to a 401(k) plan and IRA always adjust for inflation. The bottom line is that contributing to a 401(k) plan is an essential part of saving for retirement. If you change jobs, you have the several options as to what to do with your 401(k) at your previous employer.

Let's again assume that you work for XYZ Corp. but have accepted a new position as ABC Inc. For the past five years you have been contributing to XYZ's 401(k) plan and they have been giving you a 6% match dollar for dollar. Each plan is different but let's assume that after five years, you are fully vested, which means you can take everything you contributed as well as the company match even though you no longer work for XYZ Corp. Now that you work for ABC Inc. you want to begin saving in their 401(k) plan.

What do you do with the old 401(k) from XYZ Corp? You have a few options. First, you can leave it with XYZ Corp. but most likely your funds will default into the lowest risk, lowest yielding fund and will not grow at the rate that you need it to. Secondly, you have the option to potentially roll your 401(k) over into a Traditional IRA. A Traditional IRA has the same advantages as a 401(k) and you will not be subject to paying taxes or a penalty if you do so by following the rules. Thirdly, you can cash out your 401(k) and unless you absolutely, desperately need the money, this would be the last thing you should do. You would be subject to ordinary income tax and a 10% penalty if you are under the age of 59 ½ and do not qualify for an exception. Lastly, you can roll your 401(k) from XYZ Corp. (your old employer) into the 401(k) of ABC Inc. (your new employer) at usually no charge to you. You will not pay a 10% penalty, or taxes for doing this. This is usually one of the most desired options. No matter what you decide to do, remember you do have options.

If you are reading this and are considering rolling over an IRA, seek out professional help. Rules and laws change and this text should not be taken as a final guide as to how a rollover should be done. The worst thing you can do is cash out your 401(k) and pay the taxes and the penalty. If your company gives an employer match, remember that you are getting free money just for contributing to the plan. No financial advisor or stock trader anywhere in the world can beat that deal. There are other savings plans that are almost identical to a 401(k) plan known as a 403(b). 403(b)'s have the same characteristics as a 401(k).

Statistics of American Workers Who Save

Below are some statistics taken from the CRS Report for Congress by Patrick Purcell, which describes the savings patterns for certain age demographics. These statistics show that a good percentage of workers, who can participate to an employer sponsored plan, do indeed contribute. The purpose of this book is to point out that everyone should be saving, not just a "good percentage." Secondly, this book is intended to point out that the amount that we contribute needs to be increased. Most studies prove that only a fraction of those eligible to contribute to an employer sponsored plan actually contribute enough to get the full match from their employer. In essence if you do not contribute enough to get the full match, you are leaving free money "on the table." Saving in an employer sponsored plan is voluntary, which is why so few are completely educated and take full advantage of them.

Plan Participation by Employee Age

Young workers — ages 25 to 34 — are less likely than middle-aged and older workers to be employed at a firm that sponsors a retirement plan. This is because those who are younger work part time jobs and mostly at small business companies that provide no such benefits. They also are less likely to participate in retirement plans than are older workers. A greater percentage of workers aged 35 and below In 2007, 54.3% of workers 25 to 34 years old worked for an employer that sponsored a retirement plan, and 43.0% of workers in this age group participated in a company-sponsored plan. Thus, 79.2% of those aged 25 to 34 who worked for a firm that sponsored a plan participated in the plan (0.430/0.543 = 0.792). In contrast, among workers 55 to 64 years old, 63.5% worked at firms that sponsored a retirement plan, and 57.6% participated in a company-sponsored plan. Thus, among workers aged 55 to 64 who worked for a firm that sponsored a retirement plan, 90.7% participated in the plan (0.576/0.635 = 0.907).8

Plan Participation by Employee Earnings

This section shows the relationship between earnings and participation in an employer-sponsored retirement plan. Workers' annual earnings from wages and salaries — as reported on the Current Population Survey — are ranked by quartile. In 2007, one-quarter of private-sector wage and salary workers between the ages of 25 and 64 who were employed year-round, full-time earned more than $63,000. Another quarter had earnings between $40,000 and $63,000. The next quarter had earnings between $27,000 and $40,000, and those in the lowest quartile earned less than $27,000.

In 2007, 73.8% of year-round, full-time workers in the private sector with annual earnings in the top quartile were employed by firms that sponsored a retirement plan, and 69.2% of workers in the top earnings quartile participated in a retirement plan. Both of these percentages were lower than the rates in 2000 and 1995. In 2000, 80.2% of year-round, full-time workers in the private sector with annual earnings in the top quartile were employed by firms that sponsored a retirement plan, and 75.5% of workers in the top earnings quartile participated in a retirement plan. The equivalent sponsorship and participation rates in 1995 were 77.1% and 73.0%, respectively. The percentage of workers employed at firms that sponsored a retirement plan and the percentage who participated in these plans were progressively lower in each of three lowest earnings quartiles. For example, among workers in the lowest earnings quartile in 2007, 38.4% were employed at firms that sponsored a retirement plan, and 27.7% of workers in the bottom quartile participated in a retirement plan. Both of these percentages were lower than the comparable rates in 2000 and 1995. In 2000, 44.9% of year-round, full-time workers in the private sector with annual earnings in the bottom quartile were employed by firms that sponsored a retirement plan, and 32.1% of workers in the bottom earnings quartile participated in a retirement plan. The equivalent sponsorship and participation rates in 1995 were 42.4% and 30.4%, respectively. Low-wage workers are not only less likely to work for an employer that sponsors a retirement plan; they also are less likely to participate if a plan is offered. Among employees whose earnings in 2007 were in the top quartile, 73.8% worked for an employer that sponsored a retirement plan and 69.2% participated in a retirement plan. Therefore, the participation rate among employees in the top earnings quartile whose employer sponsored a retirement plan was 93.8% (0.692/0.738 = 0.938). Among workers whose 2007 earnings were in the bottom quartile, only 38.4% worked for an employer that sponsored a retirement plan and just 27.7% participated in a retirement plan. Thus, the participation rate among low wage employees whose employer sponsored a retirement plan was 72.1%.

Now that you have some idea of the percentage of people who participate and you know that those who do, most don't participate enough to at least get the full employer match, let's look at the impact of an employer match on a saving plan. Employee A is contributing 6% of his gross income to a 401(k). His employer ABC Corp. matches up to 4% of what the employee contributes. Employee A started the 401(k) at the age of 24 and will earn an average return of 8% per year. Assuming that Employee A's income stays at $40,000 his entire career (which it won't) by age 65, along with the company match, employee A will have accumulated $1,212,974. Had employee A not taken advantage of the company match at all he would have accumulated $727,784, a difference of $485,190. Knowing this information at an early age is more than half the battle. If you want to know how to get to where you're going, you need to know all the facts.

Dollar Cost Averaging

For my generation, or any generation that is not yet in retirement, the concept of dollar cost averaging (DCA) is crucial for continued success. DCA is a disciplined approach to long term investing. When you begin to save for retirement, investing in stocks, also known as equities, is imperative. Stocks have consistently proven to increase the most over the long run over any other asset class and are the only asset class to on average do better than inflation. When you invest in equities you must remember that one thing is certain, the markets will fluctuate. These market fluctuations can make investors and savers feel very uneasy. The fluctuations can make it difficult to determine the best time to buy. Another one of my sayings is that, "it's not about timing the market, it's about time in the market."

If we can safely assume that no one has a crystal ball to predict the future then we can accept the investment strategy called dollar cost averaging. DCA can help to smooth out these market fluctuations, getting rid of the need to try to invest at the best time, since we can't determine when the best time to invest is.

DCA requires that you determine a dollar amount and continually invest that dollar amount at a set time, regardless of market price. No matter if the market goes up or down dramatically, you must stay true to your set dollar amount. Because you invest a predetermined dollar amount at regular intervals, DCA makes accumulating assets convenient and efficient. Dollar cost averaging does not guarantee or ensure profit, however, DCA can help keep you from investing all of your money at one time, by forcing you to invest your money at periodic times. The key to this long term strategy is patience and consistency.

The market will rise and fall, and as it does DCA will work to your favor. Over time your average cost per share will be lower than your average price per share. The following three examples show the effects of dollar cost averaging in different types of markets. Each example assumes you regularly invest $500.

| Investment | Fluctuating Market | | |
	Amount Invested	Price	# of Shares
1	$500	10	50
2	$500	8	62
3	$500	6	83
4	$500	5	100
5	$500	8	162
Total	$2,500		357
Av.Cost/share	$7 ($2,500/357)		
Avg. Price/share	$7.40 [($10+$8+$6+	$5+$8]/5)	
Investment	Rising Market		
	Amount Invested	Price	# of Shares
1	$500	5	100
2	$500	6	83
3	$500	8	62
4	$500	8	62
5	$500	10	50
Total	$2,500		357
Av. cost/share	$7 ($2,500/357)		
Avg. Price/share	$7.40		
Investment	Falling Market		
	Amount Invested	Price	# of Shares
1	$500	10	50
2	$500	8	62

3	$500	8	62
4	$500	6	83
5	$500	5	100
Total	$2,500		357
Av.Cost/share	$7 ($2,500/357)		
Avg. Price/share	$7.40		

	Fluctuating Market		
Investment	Amount Invested	Price	# of Shares
1	$500	10	50
2	$500	8	62
3	$500	6	83
4	$500	5	100
5	$500	8	162
Total	$2,500		357
Av.Cost/share	$7 ($2,500/357)		
Avg. Price/share	$7.40 [($10+$8+$6+	$5+$8]/5)	

	Rising Market		
Investment	Amount Invested	Price	# of Shares
1	$500	5	100
2	$500	6	83
3	$500	8	62
4	$500	8	62
5	$500	10	50
Total	$2,500		357
Av. cost/share	$7 ($2,500/357)		
Avg. Price/share	$7.40		

Investment	Falling Market Amount In- vested	Price	# of Shares
1	$500	10	50
2	$500	8	62
3	$500	8	62
4	$500	6	83
5	$500	5	100
Total	$2,500		357
Av.Cost/share	$7 ($2,500/357)		
Avg. Price/ share $7.40			

Dollar cost averaging can take all the guesswork out of timing the market, which will help you accumulate more efficiently. By looking at the previous chart, we have just seen that no matter what the market fluctuation your asset accumulation will persist. Because you're buying more shares when the market declines, you will be in a better position for potential gain if and when the market rebounds. A lot of companies that offer accounts to save for retirement have a monthly accumulation plan. This is an account that automatically invests a set dollar amount each month, which you decide. This makes the process easy and seamless for the saver.

What DCA accomplishes is not letting the saver get caught up in the day to day market fluctuations that can usually make your stomach feel really uneasy by taking the emotion out of investing and saving. When you look at people who try to time the market, you will see that they usually never make money. The reason for this is because of emotion. If you use DCA you completely take the emotion out in investing and you can be confident that you will actually be better off in the long run. By "long run" I mean any period of time of ten or more years. If you are 25 and are not going to retire until 65, which is forty years away, you have a long term time horizon and DCA is a crucial aspect to your wealth accumulation.

Compound Interest

I would like people to remember me as the guy who said that "time is your number one asset." Here is a famous quote from someone you may have heard of, Albert Einstein. He said that compounding interest is the greatest power in the world. That is a bold statement coming from the mind that proved the theory of relativity. If you understand compounding interest you will begin to realize why time is out number one asset.

The more you accumulate, the more effect compounding interest will have on your accounts. It is important to remember that compounding interest can work in both ways. If your investment loses 10% then you actually need to earn 11.1% to get back to even.

Here is a simple example of this. Assume you own a stock that is worth $100 and it loses 10% taking your investment down to a value of $90. In order to get back to your original $100 you need to earn $10. $10 on what is now $90 is actually 11.1%. So it is important to realize that compounding interest is powerful in both directions.

Taking a different approach of compounding interest, we ask the question, "Why can it be so effective?" This simple example should help you see why. Assume that you have two investments and for the sake of this example we will name them A and B. Investment A is worth $1,000 and investment B is worth $1,000,000. Let's also assume that you earn the same 10% rate of return on both investments. 10% on $1,000 is $100, so your total value for investment A is now $1,100. That same 10% on investment B earned you $100,000. So your total value for investment B is now $1,100,000. We see that the same 10% was earned on both investments but investment B had a much more dramatic impact because of the original value of the account.

Looking at it this way, the difference is obvious. When you save for an entire lifetime you build your savings and retirement accounts up as big as you can so that you can take advantage of compounding interest later in life when it has a much more potent impact. If you begin saving in your twenties or earlier, your accounts have the ability to grow much bigger, thus allowing you to take advantage of the power of compounding interest. If you wait until later in life to start saving, you miss out on the power of compounding interest and do not get to use it to its full advantage.

This is why I say that time is our number one asset. The earlier you begin to save, the more you can build up, which allows you the opportunity to take full advantage of the power of compounding interest.

Let me describe for you one more quick example of the power of compounding interest. For this example we will assume that both investors "Rich" and "Poor" earn the same 10% rate of return annually on their investments.

Investor "Rich" begins saving $50 a month while in college and it takes him five years too finish. "Poor" saves nothing each month while in college, instead stating that he will wait until he gets done with school to start saving. By the time "Rich" graduates five years later, he has accumulated almost $4,200. They are both 25 and recently graduated from college and "Rich" accumulated almost $4,200 and "Poor" has $0.

After graduation both "Rich" and "Poor" invest $50 each month and earn the same 10% rate of return annually from age 25 until age 65. At age 65 "Rich" has accumulated roughly $297,000 and "Poor" has accumulated roughly $182,000. That is a difference of $115,000.

Remember how each started out? "Rich" invested $50 a month while in college and "Poor" did not. Upon graduation "Rich" had $4,200 and because of compounding interest over the next 35 years, "Rich" ended up with almost $115,000 more. Now it is easy to see why Einstein called compounding interest the greatest power in the universe. The reason "Rich" was able to accumulate so much more was because he started earlier. "Rich" did not contribute thousands of dollars at a time, he just contributed small amounts but on a consistent basis and for longer period of time than "Poor".

Today "Poor" and "Rich" get together and talk about their retirement portfolios and "Rich" always reminds "Poor" that he should have saved $50 a month while in college. "Poor" wishes he could turn back the hands in time and do it all over again. "Poor" now realizes, even though it is too late, that he made a huge mistake.

Other than the fact that "Rich" started five years earlier, the two investors did exactly the same thing and each got the same return on their investment. Time is our number one asset, and I hope you are beginning to see why I say this. Start early, contribute on a regular basis (i.e. once a month) and take advantage of the power of compounding interest.

Saving $1 Million Dollars

So you want to be a millionaire? What does it realistically take these days to accumulate $1 million dollars? We discussed earlier that for our generation $1 million in savings will not be enough. However, we will take a look at several different scenarios to see what needs to be done to accumulate that amount. You need to then realize that $1 million will not be enough so you may consider saving even more or accounting for increased wages and income.

Accumulating a million dollars depends on three very important factors: the amount you contribute, the rate of return you achieve and the length of time you contribute for. Two of the three variables we can control and the third we have no control over. The two that we can control are the amount we contribute and the length of time we contribute. The factor that we cannot control is the return we achieve on our investment, making this the variable factor.

Let's take a look at eight different investors and their savings habits throughout their lives. Each investor will earn the same 10% return on investment average per year, for illustration purposes.

Investor # 1 starts investing at age 20. Investor #1 will need to contribute $1,256/year, $104/month for 45 years to accumulate $1 million dollars by age 65. Notice that that is a total contribution over the 45 years of $56,520.

Investor # 2 starts investing at age 25. Investor #2 will need to contribute $2,045/year, $170/month for 40 years to accumulate $1 million dollars by age 65. Notice that that is a total contribution over the 40 years of $81,800.

Investor # 3 starts investing at age 30. Investor #3 will need to contribute $3,350/year, $279/month for 35 years to accumulate $1 million dollars by age 65. Notice that that is a total contribution over the 35 years of $117,250.

Investor # 4 starts investing at age 35. Investor #4 will need to contribute $5,560/year, $463/month for 30 years to accumulate $1 million dollars by age 65. Notice that that is a total contribution over the 30 years of $166,800.

Investor # 5 starts investing at age 40. Investor #5 will need to contribute $9,300/year, $775/month for 25 years to accumulate $1 million dollars by age 65. Notice that that is a total contribution over the 25 years of $232,500.

Investor # 6 starts investing at age 45. Investor #6 will need to contribute $15,900/year, $1,325/month for 20 years to accumulate $1 million dollars by age 65. Notice that that is a total contribution over the 20 years of $318,000.

Investor # 7 starts investing at age 50. Investor #7 will need to contribute $28,600/year, $2,383/month for 15 years to accumulate $1 million dollars by age 65. Notice that that is a total contribution over the 15 years of $429,000.

Investor # 8 starts investing at age 55. Investor #8 will need to contribute $57,100/year, $4,758/month for 10 years to accumulate $1 million dollars by age 65. Notice that that is a total contribution over the 10 years of $571,000.

To recap, Investor #1 invested a total out of pocket contribution of only $56,520 to accumulate $1 million, while Investor #8 invested a total out of pocket contribution of

$571,000, which a difference of $514,480 to accumulate the same $1 million dollars. Which would you prefer to do?

The longer you wait to start saving the more you will have to contribute out of your own pocket to potentially break even. Saving for retirement and investing for the long term is not hard, you just need to be discipline enough to do so.

Remember that there are three factors involved: contributions, length of time invested and return on investment. Also remember that you can only control two out of the three. Your account value will constantly change on how these three variables are controlled. If you increase your contribution you have the potential to reach your goal sooner, which would decrease your amount of time before you reach your goal. Your return on investment will fluctuate, causing your account to always be different.

Now you know what is possible, so get out there and set up a plan to start saving and you can become a millionaire some day too. If you take my stance and believe that $1 million will not be enough, then do things to accumulate more than $1 million. This example gives you an idea of the magnitude of savings and time to accomplish your goals. It will not happen over night, but you can reach your goal if you are discipline.

There are plans out there that allow you to contribute on a monthly basis automatically and electronically. This allows your monthly contributions to be automatic, discipline, smart, effortless and always on time, so take advantage of them.

Talking With 3 Millionaires

I sat down with three self made millionaires and asked them to describe characteristics that define themselves and how they view other millionaires behavior patterns. Not too surprisingly, all three millionaires described similar characteristics about what made them successful and what they see in other successful people. The following is the cliff notes version of what the three millionaires divulged and I have broken their responses down into ten themes.

1. ***Don't care about what others think of you based on material things.*** Don't worry that your neighbor sees you driving a ten year old vehicle. Don't worry about the fact that you're not living in a bigger house than your best friend. In today's age, we as a society are so obsessed with the house we live in and the car that we drive, and we shouldn't be. Don't worry that your spouse does not have the elegant jewelry fancy shoes that her friends have. If your friends and the people that are close to you judge you for these reasons, then maybe they are not your friends. The vehicles that each of these millionaires drive are; Chevy Pickup truck, Chevy Malibu sedan and Dodge Caravan, hardly luxury cars by any means. Each of these individuals can easily afford major luxury brands, however, they say one of the characteristics of being a millionaire is getting rid of the notion about what others think of you based on material things.

2. ***Be Patient.*** Patience is a virtue. This theme was touched on by all three millionaires. Very few people get wealthy over night. Some people get rich over night, only to lose it all. Instead of focusing on the things that may get you rich quickly, focus on the things that will get you wealthy over the long term. Vehicles such as IRA's, employer sponsored plans and real estate. Notice they did not say things such as boats, cars and electronics. This is a characteristic that the millionaires saw in themselves and in other successful people. Good things come to those who are patient.

3. ***Set Goals Both Short and Long Term***. Each millionaires mentioned that people are more likely to succeed if they set goals. It is not enough to just think

of a goal or set a goal, but to write them down. They recommended putting the goal that you have written down in a place where you will see it frequently. Even though setting a long term goal is important, even more so is setting short term goals to accomplish on your way to your long term goal. Going along with the previous characteristics of being patient, things are rarely done overnight. Setting short term goals motivate you to get to your long term goal. If you accomplish a short term goal you can become motivated to reach the next goal as opposed to being stuck in the "middle" of a long term goal. Think of these short term goals as baby steps. A short term goal could be to save $50 a month while in school with a long term goal of saving a total of $5,000 while in school for five years. This will force you to save a little more than your $50 a month. Setting goals, in the minds of the millionaires, is a vital characteristic.

4. ***Start Early and Contribute Often.*** While the three millionaires are invested in many savings vehicles, they stressed the importance of starting early. When you begin at an early age, you are setting the ground work for a lifetime of growth. At the core of this growth potential is the power of compounding which can do its job better the longer you have contributed. Contributions are imperative for building wealth. Contributing right after you get paid forces you, (and if you are like me, it is tempting to spend the money if it is there) to contribute to the accounts that are most important. When you make more money, as your career advances, contribute more. One millionaire said, "I was extremely lucky to learn at an early age to set aside what I could afford to, and now that I am older I am so thankful for the sacrifices I made through my life to get to where I am today."

5. ***Learn Lessons The Hard Way Otherwise You May Not Learn Them.*** Hardships and failures are bound to happen in everyone's lifetime. Whether it's early on in life, midlife or as a senior citizen, we will all fall on challenging times. It was said by one millionaire, "If I could choose, I would have all my failures out of the way early on in life, because I get them out of the way." Obviously we can't choose when we fail, but learning by your own mistakes and the mistakes of others will greatly open your eyes to great life lessons. Do not be afraid to take a calculated risk. Do not be afraid of failure, it will only make you stronger in the long run.

6. ***Become Properly Educated.*** Getting a high school, college, and graduate level education is more important now than ever before. Getting a good education to get a good job is considered by many as the American dream. They argue that it is just as important that we get an education on the topics of saving and investing in our own financial future. A student can easily go through more than 20 years of education and not learn one thing about planning for what to do after work. Become educated on all of your options and plans. Sometimes it is not the most exciting thing to do and many people will not do it even though they know they should. Since our education system currently has little to no coverage on saving and investing education, you are encouraged to research on your own all the options that you have. It will be some of the most valuable information you will ever receive.

7. ***Give Back To Others.*** The most successful people in the world have one thing in common, they give back. Their vast fortunes allow them to do so, but giving back, no matter what the scale or scope is an important characteristic of successful people. The act

of giving will come back to you in so many ways. Individuals, business and corporations are so thankful for those who give to the less fortunate. It is important to realize that those who are generous and give back what they can will be rewarded in some way because what goes around comes around.

8. ***Lose The Bad Financial Habits.*** This is much easier said than done. Bad financial habits are the small things that we do in our daily lives that make it harder to build wealth. Our bad financial habits siphon money out of our pockets. The millionaires encourage you to think about if you were to stop just one bad habit at $3 a day and earmark that money to an interest bearing account. Using their example, an individual that saves $3 a day to an interest bearing account at 5% over the course of 35 years will grow to $104,000. No one is here to tell you how to live your life or the decisions you should make, rather we are here to say that if saving enough for retirement is important to you, then make some changes. If taking advice from three millionaires who are telling you that changing bad financial habits is a characteristic of building wealth, then decide for you if it's worth making some changes. Bad financial habits add up. If I told you that you could accumulate $104,000 by stopping one bad habit a day, would you do it?

9. ***Work Harder Than The "Next Guy."*** Work ethic is something that can be learned. Having a strong and healthy work ethic is a core value that millionaires possess. If your work colleagues get to work at 8am, you should get there at 7am. If they leave work at 5pm, you should stay there until 6pm. Continue to work hard and it will get noticed. You will not need to tell people that you are working hard, but they will see your work ethic come out as time goes on. Stick to your own business and it will show. The millionaires

stress that it is important to find work that you enjoy doing, and it will not seem like work. It will not be "work" if you have to go out of town or work weekends or holidays to get the job done. They stressed that you need to find what you love, and work like hell. Those who are successful work the hardest. One of the millionaires owns many real estate properties. These properties are his primary residence and the house on each side of him. Each lot is about 2 acres and this millionaire constantly works on the properties himself. He can easily pay a worker to come in and do all the work for him, but even still into his 70's he gets out there and gets his hands dirty. He is continuing to work harder than most people his age, not because he has to but because he believes in this value. One of the millionaires pointed out that if your boss needs to make a decision as to who to give the promotion to, they will seriously consider work ethic. If your boss knows that you come in early, stay late and are committed to your job, all other things being equal, you are more prone to getting the promotion. If you work for yourself, your work ethic will define your business and your reputation. Continue to work harder than the "next guy" and good things are bound to come your way.

10. *Surround Yourself With Like Minded People.* Each millionaire suggested that it is very important to surround yourself with people that have a positive influence and attitude. You are better off associating with people who are where you want to be. These people that you associate with will help give you direction that you may not even know about. They are not going out late at night, and skipping work. They are not procrastinating and they do not have a negative attitude towards things. It is very easy to get down on yourself when things are not going your way.

It is important to continue to surround yourself with positive people. All the millionaires stated that successful people love to help others. They say that those types of people remind them of themselves. They love working and helping people who have ambition, are willing to take a calculated risk, who work hard and like to learn. Do not be afraid to seek out help from successful people. Even though they may be busy, successful people love to extend a helping hand when they can. The millionaires suggested that you look for a mentor who does what it is you think you will want to do with your life and ask them to teach you some lessons on life, family and business. Whither you want to be a teacher, firefighter, entrepreneur or pilot, we can all use the help of others. Continue to surround yourself with people who are like you.

Estate Planning Strategy Using Life Insurance

The following are estate planning strategies you can use early on in life to try to achieve accumulating greater assets using life insurance. Life Insurance is a term that most people cringe at when they hear it. When I hear the term, I think of opportunity. You might be saying to yourself, how do you see opportunity in life insurance? Well there are ways to use life insurance to your benefit and if you are educated on it, and decide to take action, you can greatly benefit from it. There are a couple different ways this benefit can work and I will explain them both right now.

Case #1.

For this to work, you need someone; mom, dad, grandma, grandpa or uncle Joe to have some extra money sitting aside that they know they will not need in their life. They know they want to do something good with the money but are not sure what. For the sake of this example, let's assume that it is mom who has the extra money sitting around. The $40,000 that mom has can be used to buy what is called an annuity. An annuity has a feature on it that allows mom to receive a guaranteed amount of income for the rest of her life. The amount of money that is received each year depends on the age mom is when she purchases the annuity. In this example let's say that mom is 55 years old. She is entitled to receive 5.5% of her original investment amount, which was $40,000, every year from the annuity company for the rest of her life. 5.5% of $40,000 is $2,200 a year in income. This may not seem like a whole lot to you, but what you do with that income is the important part.

The next step is to get mom, who is healthy, to purchase a life insurance policy on herself with you as the beneficiary, using the $2,200 a year she gets from the annuity to fund the premium. Mom has just bought a life insurance policy and can fully fund the premium every year for the rest of her life.

Mom applies for, and because she is healthy, gets an approval for $400,000 in death benefit from the life insurance policy. This means that when mom dies (and everyone dies at some time) the beneficiary, which is you, will receive $400,000 in death benefit. Life insurance proceeds, such as the one in this example, are income tax free. So what you have just done is took $40,000 that mom did not need anyway and turned it into $400,000 tax-free! Since mom named you as beneficiary of the annuity, you are also entitled to the value of the annuity upon mom's death. The annuity is taxed at your ordinary income level, but the life insurance death benefit that is paid to you is not. Not a bad way to make great use of funds that mom was planning on passing on anyway.

Case #2.

We will use the same numbers as in the example above, but this time there is no money from mom or dad, you need to fund this one on your own. Remember that mom is 55 and in good health and hopefully she lives to see 100. Since there is no $40,000 to purchase the annuity, like in the previous example, you need to come up with $2,200 a year to fund the life insurance policy yourself. $2,200 a year is $183 a month. If that is too much for you to handle, get a sibling to split the cost with you. Let's assume though that you can afford the $2,200 a year premium on mom's life insurance policy. Since mom is 55 and in good health, she is able to qualify for a life insurance policy that will pay a death benefit to the beneficiary, which is you, of $400,000. Even if mom lives to age 100, which we hope she does, you would have paid out $99,000 in premiums over the course of that 45 year span. If mom dies at 100, you will receive the $400,000 death benefit, income tax free! If you subtract from the $400,000 the $99,000 you paid in premium over the course of the last 45 years, you have still netted $301,000, which again is income tax free. The theory behind this strategy works best as in Case #1, but it is something to think about. The power of knowing that a strategy like this exists is tremendous. Assuming you are in the 25% tax bracket you would have to accumulate $376,250 over that 45 year time span to breakeven with this strategy.

Life insurance death benefits are income tax free to the beneficiary. To accumulate $376,250 over the 45 year time span and accumulating the $2,200 a year you would have to earn a rate of return of 5.1% every year for 45 straight years. If mom only lives 10 years from the date of buying the insurance policy you would have to earn a 50% return per year to equal the same benefit you would get from the insurance policy. Again, this is a strategy that works best with extra money, like in the scenario of Case #1, but Case #2 gives you something to think about.

So if you know about this strategy, and it is suitable for you and your situation why not utilize it? Take the idea for what it is worth. This is an idea that your kids, if and when you have any, would absolutely love you for. Start in your early twenties setting aside $20 a week or $1,040 a year. Put that money into an account that will grow at a conservative level of say 4% per year. If you start doing this at age 20 and continue to let it grow until you are 60 that money would grow to roughly $102,000. At the age of 60, use this strategy that we just discussed and use the funds to buy an annuity that will pay you 6% interest income for the rest of your life. 6% of $102,000 is $6,120, which can be used to fund the premium on a $1,000,000 life insurance policy. Make your children the beneficiaries and you have just created a $1,000,000 tax free asset to them upon your death just by setting aside $20 a week.

This type of strategy may be necessary going forward in the future. Just think about if your parents had done this for you since the time they were in their twenties. I wish I could say that I had something like this waiting for me. Our generation needs to think outside the box and do things differently than our parents did. There are things we can do, we just need to have the education to know how to do them.

Buying a Primary Residence or Investment Property

Prior to the age of 24 I had bought and sold over $470,000 worth of real estate. Some of it was investment property, some of it was for primary residence and some of it was rental property. One of the real estate deals I made completely changed my life and was a terrible experience, however, I will never forget the experience and I have learned a tremendous amount from my mistakes in real estate.

The reason I am writing about real estate is because there are many factors in real estate that can be beneficial when putting a financial plan together. I also understand that as a college student or young professional, buying a home may be in your near future.

The purpose for this book is to talk about how you can use the interest on a loan to lower your tax burden each year. I would not recommend that you buy a property solely for the tax benefits you receive, however, if you are in the position to buy property, consider the benefits that go along with property ownership. I am not going to talk about how to get rich quick buying and selling real estate, and I am not going to talk about the negatives of investing in real estate such as property taxes, insurance, declining values and exotic mortgages.

If you are younger and a first time home buyer, whether it be for your primary residence or investment property, consider the option of a mortgage or leverage. Lending standards will always change based on the condition of the industry and economy, but typically a low risk borrower (someone trying to obtain a loan) will need cash for a down payment and a good credit score (something in the 650-800 range). If and when you get approved for a loan and buy property, keep in mind this advantage.

If you choose itemized deductions, instead of the standard deduction, you get to deduct or itemize the interest you pay on your loan each year. You can use this tax law with a loan on a primary residence, investment property or even a home equity line of credit. Let's take a look at a very basic example on how this might be beneficial. The following numbers are not accurate according to current tax laws and should not be viewed as such. They are used simply for illustrative purposes. Assume you get a standard deduction from the IRS on your taxes this year of $5,000. That means that you can deduct $5,000 from your taxable income in that year. This is not a dollar for dollar credit, instead it is a deduction. So if your total income for this year is $45,000, you get to automatically deduct $5,000 and report to the IRS income of $40,000 of taxable income.

Now lets assume that you close on a new house for your primary residence on January 1st of this year and your monthly mortgage payment equals $1,000 a month. Of that $1,000 monthly payment, $850 is interest paid on the loan. Remember you need to pay interest on money you borrow. At the end of the year your lender will send you a statement stating that you paid $10,200 ($850 a month * 12 months) in interest during the year.

Since $10,200 is more than your standard deduction of $5,000 you can elect to use what is called an itemized deduction and reduce your taxable income by $10,200 for that year. Now we take your income of $45,000 and subtract your interest paid to the lender of $10,200 and you have reduced your taxable income to $34,800. Assuming that you pay a flat tax rate of 20 % and ignoring marginal tax rates for illustrative purposes and no other tax consequences exist, your total tax liability has been reduced from $8,000 (that is 20% tax on $40,000) to $6,960 (which is 20% tax on $34,800). You have now reduced your taxable income by $5,200 and have saved yourself $1,040 in taxes.

A tax consultant should be contacted to help you with the fine tuning to this tax law. Again, do not use this solely as a means to go out and buy property. If you are in a position to buy real estate, consider this tax law and use it to your advantage. Tax law is forever changing so before using this information, please consult a tax professional.

Thank You and Congratulations

I would like to thank you and congratulate you for taking the time to read this book and I hope that you have taken something from it. By taking these concepts and putting them to good use, you have decided to take your own financial future into your hands. You have done what most baby boomers wish they had done years ago and read a book that described to them that saving, even at an early age, is so important. It does not matter if you make a moderate income. Great things can be accomplished with small contributions and persistent action. I would like to recap the main themes of this book one last time and ask that if you don't take anything else from this book that you take this out of it.

Theme #1:

The times have changed, we need to change too. The times are constantly changing and if you believe this to be true then the solutions of the past are no longer a useful reference. Our generation needs to plan for retirement differently than any generation before us. Gigantic hurdles are coming our way and we need to prepare for them as early on as we can. Planning does not take much time or effort. All it takes is a little knowledge and an understanding that the times are changing.

Please understand that we cannot afford to have the same saving and spending habits as the generations before us. We have grown accustom to thinking that we can have instant gratification, and that needs to be reversed. We as a generation need to save more often and we need to learn how to sacrifice. No one else is out there talking to my generation, so I decided I would. The times have changed, we need to change too to keep up.

Theme #2:

Get educated, and do it before your 25th birthday. Getting this education before your 25th birthday, if not earlier, is a crucial part of developing a great plan. Starting this early, or even earlier, will give you the potential to accumulate more wealth. The earlier you become educated on matters of retirement planning, the earlier you can take action, which in turn gives you the potential to build a greater nest egg.

The average American begins saving at age 40. I am not sure if this is due to lack of education or lack of taking action. What I do know is that if you wait until 40 to begin saving, you will have some major catch up to play. Our education system, as of 2008, does not provide much information on retirement planning. Unfortunately, our generation is missing out on one of the greatest educations of all, the education on saving and realizing the times have changed and retirement planning needs to start a lot earlier than we think. If you don't believe me, just ask any baby boomer that have saved $25,000 or less. Ask them if they would do things differently if they could start over? Ask them if they wish they had got this education before their 25th birthday and took action on it? We need to become educated on the correct topics and then ultimately take action.

Theme #3:

I became frustrated with the lack of scattered resources for our generation. Just because we have 30 or 40 years until retirement doesn't mean that we can't think about or plan for it. Most "professionals" do not want to educate my generation because we are not the "big account" bringing in the $1,000,000 accounts. Many financial advisors will tell you this. They view my generation as a waste of time. I see great potential in my generation and I also see virtually no one educating them on these important matters. I feel a fiduciary and moral obligation to dedicate my work towards educating and helping my generation. With the launch of financialyoung.com, my generation and the generations to follow now have a starting point with which to get educated and begin to take action. This book, in my opinion, is just as important as any text book you will read in high school or college. There is now a place for us to get educated, informed and inspired.

Theme #4:

You don't need a lot of money to start and that you can't afford to wait any longer to begin. All it takes to begin is $50. As we have seen many times in this book, $50 a month, early on, can make a huge difference over the long tem. We all have long term time horizons and time is our number one asset. By starting earlier, we can potentially take much greater advantage of the power of compounding interest, later in life. For this reason alone, you can't afford to wait any longer to begin. Many of us can afford to set aside and save $50 a month. My generation does not do so because no one is telling them they must. If it were up to me, I would make it a law that all high school students, providing they have a job, have to save $50 a month into a retirement account. This would force them to save. Making it mandatory to save, at an early age, would be the best thing for this generation. It would force us to fatten our own pockets. I know there are many thoughts against this, but my point is not to try to change laws, rather it is to point out the things that are of great importance and starting to save at an early age is one of them.

Theme #5:

The Not so Fantastic 4. Without going into great detail again about these four major problems our generation will face, remember they will challenge our generation and that they will be our reality someday. The day will come where we will wake up and it is going to hit us. Boom, I'm eligible to receive Social Security benefits, am I even going to get anything? Boom, I am 65, is my old employer going to provide me with a pension? Boom, I'm retired and my health and medical benefits went down and my costs went up, did I prepare for this to happen? These are things we will all one day need to ask ourselves. Will we be ready when these bombshells hit? Will we be ready to live a life of retirement into our 90's or even 100's? Will we be able to afford it? What kind of help will we get from the government? What will I have done to prepare for it? Am I going to have to rely on someone else to take care of me financially? These are serious questions to answer. Just like society asks a young twenty something what they want to do, career wise, for the rest of their life, we now need to ask these same twenty something's to start planning for retirement. Wither you think it is fair or not, it is our reality. The Not so Fantastic 4 are coming and either you will be prepared or you won't, it is up to you to decide.

Theme #6:

Don't end up a bad statistic. Statistics have shown that the baby boomer generation on average did a poor job of saving for retirement. In fact, the average baby boomer has only saved roughly $60,000. 40% of this generation has saved $25,000 or less. Is that what you want to be remembered by? Do you want to work until you are forced to retire due to your health? Many will end up like this but it does not need to be like this for our generation. Instead, learn about what can be done at an early age and take action. Be proactive in becoming a good statistic, one who has accumulated enough for retirement and the high medical costs our generation will face coupled with longer life expectancies. Our generation does not need to end up a bad statistic, so don't let it happen.

Theme #7:

Start Saving Now! It is as simple as that. Beginning to save early in life is the key point of this book. Remember that time is our greatest asset and once today is gone you can never get it back. I understand that we all have so many things going on in our lives. I understand that the thought of retirement, being 30 or 40 years away, is hard to fathom. I understand that you may be more interested in sports, girls, boys, music or the science club, but some emphasis needs to be put on retirement planning at an early age. Try not to let another day pass you by without taking some action towards saving.

Up to now, the only way our generation knows about the importance of saving is if a friend or family member told them or they did their own independent research. There are resources available to you that are both easy to understand and get involved in. If times are tough for you right now, continue to stick it out and work hard towards making changes. Will you be prepared when the great changes that are coming eventually do arrive? Will you plan for the changes that are taking place right now?

Our generation must work together and help, support and educate each other. Our parents' generation does not give a damn about us, they care about themselves, for if they did care, they would not have mortgaged our future and piled up so much debt. It is time that we as a generation unite and put our future in our own hands. It is time that we make the changes necessary to survive. It is time that we understand that we will face major challenges. It is time to tackle those challenges head on, right now. The time is now, to learn and act right now.

I hope you enjoyed this book and that you found some of the information useful. I hope that you were inspired to take action and plan for the future even though society doesn't tell us to. I hope that you have learned that the time to put your financial future in your own hands is now. Ask anyone who has not saved enough, if they would do things differently if they could go back and all of them would say "yes." Don't make the same mistakes and don't say the same thing when you turn 65.

I encourage you to visit financialyoung.com for information and tools that are always being updated with the changing times. My goal with this book was to open your eyes on the challenges our generation and future generations will face and to shed light on the fact that the times are changing and we need to as well. I wish you the best in all that you do, and remember Start Saving Now!

Sample Action Plan:

Monthly Income	$4,000
Employer Sponsored Plan	$400
IRA monthly contribution	$400
Fixed Monthly Expenses	$1,800
Variable Monthly Expenses	$500
Entertainment Funds	$200
Monthly Reserve Funds	$700

Questions to consider:

What good would answering these questions at age 40, 50, or 60 be if you have not answered them early on in life and already began to prepare for them?

In _____months from now, I see myself doing

_____.

In _____ months from now, I see myself saving _____ a month.

My goal is to save (set aside in retirement accounts) $ _____ this year.

Right now I am saving _____.

After going to financialyoung.com and reviewing the calculators, I should be saving _____.

My shortfall/surplus is _____. (retirement planning calculator)

I am on track to save $_____ by the time I am 65. (retirement planning calculator)

What will I do if income (for whatever reason) does not come in for 6 months? _____.

I have _____ months of reserve money in case I lose my income.

I have $_____ saved up as reserve money.

_____ is an expense I could eliminate and use that money towards savings.

That money will come to $ _____ extra a month.

I have set up a Roth IRA and am contributing $ _____ a month.

I have set up my 401(k) at work and am contributing $ _____ a month.

My employer contributes up to _____% of my contribution into my 401(k) each month.

I have _____ out of the possible 4 branches to the retirement planning tree already set up.

When do I plan to retire or expect to need income to supplement my retirement?

How much will I need in addition to other sources of retirement income?

Will I be able to afford the retirement I want?

How much investment risk am I comfortable with?

I want to retire by the age of _____, which occurs in _____ years.

What is your greatest financial challenge today?

What is your greatest financial fear?